THE DOOR OF THE HOLY OF HOLIES IN ADDIS ABABA CATHEDRAL

ETHIOPIAN PRIESTS CARRYING THE TABLETS OF THE TEN COMMANDMENTS

Ethiopia
And the Missing Link in
African History

BY

REV. STERLING M. MEANS

Published by

Lushena Books

1804-06 West Irving Park Road
Chicago, IL 60613

TEL: 773-975-9945
FAX: 773-975-0045

ISBN 0-94839-030-1

*Artists Conception
by
Charles Pridgen*

**BIBLE REFERENCE:
REVELATIONS 1:14-15**

Dedicated to my many white and colored friends in the States of Ohio and Pennsylvania who have encouraged and helped me in my program to lift the colored race.

Author of

THE DESERTED CABIN

———

THE GERMAN WAR LORD AND THE BRITISH LION

———

THE BLACK DEVILS AND OTHER POEMS

———

AFRICA AND THE WORLD PEACE

FOREWORD

My purpose in writing this volume was inspired by observations and research in surveying the serious economic conditions that confront the Negro of today in the most confused and complicated crisis that has ever challenged human intelligence.

One of the causes that led to my research was that, heretofore, the problem in the main was political and social, but in recent years, it has become economic and "job-finding." I have found, in research, that the problem was more serious than politics or job-finding; and as I proceeded further, I discovered it was not even a problem, but rather the most misguided system of race relation in the world, which affects every vital phase of American life, namely: political, economic, social and religious activities of her Commonwealth and tends to make America the greatest make-believe people on earth.

The Black Race has been miseducated about itself and misguided by its leaders. For the past fifty years, with only two exceptions, the Race has not been given the true facts about its history and its future.

Millions of dollars have been spent on the education of its youth, yet with all the schools and colleges, we still have a problem or, in a more practical sense, what *they* call a problem. The lack of proper education is the fundamental handicap to a solution. This is largely due to the knowledge obtained from books written about the race and its African Fatherland.

These books which are written by men of learning but often prompted by selfish and prejudicial motives, make the Negro the sub-strata of the Human Race—an "Inferior Race," a Hewer of wood; and a drawer of water, and the most ungainly group in the realm of mankind, hardly human.

These books published by big publishing houses, with vast circulations, find their way into City, College and High School libraries. These books give the youth a confused complex of the race, with no practical approach to its problem and no objective for its future.

The only background that the colored youth gets of itself in the textbook is slavery and the wilds of the African Jungle, which makes the native a sub-human, an out-cast in society and an alien to the commonwealth of international Brotherhood.

These prejudiced authors strive their utmost to defame the history and anthropology of the African people, by using such terms as Negro, Negroid, Nigritic, Negress, Nigger, Negreto and Negrillo. These names have become official terms to support their false and prejudiced hypotheses.

On the other hand, I am not overlooking the fact that there are yet some very outstanding historians and anthropologists, who dare to tell the truth; while others of them just tell enough facts and leave the rest half disclosed, so that one can rarely draw an elaborate conclusion. These authors are the ones upon which a great deal of my argument will largely depend to substantiate the facts in African History, not familiarly known to the reading public.

The vast majority of recent writers on African History and travels, try to exclude the Negro from his African History, and the achievements of its civilization wrought in the past and vainly try to give the credit to some other race.

This was strikingly noticed during the Italian-Ethiopian War. Some of the leading writers, commentators, and college professors, in their reference to Ethiopia, would say, "They are not Negroes"! Then, I became more concerned about the History of the Black Race than ever and began to look for its missing link. This I have found and in this volume have welded it together; and in so doing, it projects a solution for the problem in America and a redemption of the African continent.

Such words as Problem and Negro, Negroid and Negretto, will only be used in this volume for the convenience of argument, accommodative but not in a genetic sense. The Black Race has no problem and there is no such Race as Negro, Negroid, and Negreto; but since they have become popular usages, I only use them to accommodate custom and to prove the false existence of their claim. This is the reason why the so-called Race Problem has not been solved, as the Race has not found itself. It is lost, lost in the wilderness of a misguided system of education and a misguided leadership.

The object and aim of this volume is to show them the solution in the light of History, that they may find their own way; in the words of our Saviour—"And Ye Shall Know The Truth, And The Truth Shall Make You Free."

CONTENTS

LIST OF ILLUSTRATIONS

THE CALL OF AFRICA

Africa is calling thee,
Far across the deep blue sea,
Where her ancient rivers run,
In the land of tropic sun;
How can you contented be?
Africa is calling thee!

There beneath the African blue,
Harvest great, laborers few;
Will you heed Macedonian call,
Jesus Christ, He died for all;
Hear the cry beyond the sea,
Africa is calling thee!

Zion's Watchmen sound alarms,
In the groves of fronded palms,
Let Ethiopia now awake,
Let Sahara's silence break,
With the Gospel Jubilee,
Africa is calling thee!

Holy Child of Bethlehem,
Africa rescued Him;
He Whom Herod sought to slay—
He Whom Pilate tried one day,
She bore His cross to Calvary
Now Africa is calling thee!

1

The Coming of the Black Men

"Art Thou The First Man That Was Born, Or Wast Thou Made Before The Hills?"—Job 15-7

I have often been asked by the friends of the Black Race—"Where did the Negro come from; and what was really the cause of his complexion and texture of hair?" They were really sincere in their questions and really wanted to know. The reason for this is that popular historians have left the Black Race without a common brotherhood and have cut the branch of the tree from which he sprung and severed the link in the ascending chain of Racial evolution.

They readily talk about branch and blood of all the races of mankind; yet they exclude the Negro and rather place him on the lowest scale of the human family. When it comes to the description of other races, they give their direct origin such as, the White race, is known as an Indo-European race, and other nations such as Jews, Arabs, Turks, Chinese, Japanese and other Asiatic and Pacific nations; even the American Indians are known as Semites. These biased writers invade Africa, divide the African nation into separate units, using such terms as Hamités and Negroes. They also claim that Egyptians, Ethiopians, Berbers, Libyans are . . . are brunettes or dark whites. They speak of the Negroes as a separate and inferior race and say that from time immemorial have been hewers of wood and drawers of water for their more fortunate brethren. That the Negro has neither built a Stone City nor suggested a Creed.

While these historians admit that the race belongs to the Human family, without a direct connection, they evade the expression, but nevertheless, they use the argument by saying, "That the Negro is the only 'race' that does not have a tradition of the Flood." The Negro is not classified as an Indo-European, neither as a Semite nor even a Hamite. What is he? "We are positive that there are but three Races in a generic sense namely: The Hamite, the European, and the Semite. Other races are just secondary or subsidiary races belonging to these respective stocks. Ham today is classified as "White," but during the days of slavery he was very "Black."

The so-called Christian nations, that tolerated slavery, bolstered their conscience by saying that it was a decree from the curse of Noah, and that the Black Race, a descendant of Ham, should be a slave as a fulfillment of Noah's curse; and because Ham laughed at his father's nakedness while he was in a drunken stupor, Noah said, "Cursed be Canaan, a servant of servant shall he be unto his brethren." During the days of slavery, Ham was considered a "Black" man; in 1861, Jefferson Davis, in his famous speech indorsing secession of states, referred to the Negro as the "Son of Ham"; during the Italian-Ethiopian war in 1935, "Ham" was considered a brunette White man in the Northern and Eastern part of Africa. South of the Sahara, his descendants were classified as Negroes but not "Hamites." Such arguments are not even good jokes to intelligent people.

On the other hand, if Noah's curse had affected the course of Hamitic History, it would have fallen on the posterity of Canaan and not the so-called Negro since the ancestor of the Ethiopian or Negro race was Cush, another son of "Ham"—yet the curse was on Canaan.

Dr. Blyden says in his book, "Liberia's Offering," that the prophecy would have been fulfilled when the Jews, under the leadership of Joshua, invaded Canaan and conquered the Canaanites and made them their servants, when they, the Jews, had been slaves or servants to the Egyptians (Hamites), which fulfilled the prophecy as "Servant of Servants."

This subhuman relation has another expression in the children of white and black parents. They are called Mulatto or Hybrid, but children between white and Indians and other dark races are termed as half-breeds. It is also claimed that these Mulattoes become sterile in the third generation, which supports a theory that the difference between the white and black is similar to the relation between horse and mule. This is not true, for I have seen Octoroons, with seven or eight children in their family, so white until you could not tell where "Ham" left off and Japheth started. If this theory

[3]

was true, the handicap would be in the first generation where the resistance would be greater. The Mulatto is not a hybrid like a mule. He reproduces like any other human; in fact, there are no such groups as Mulattoes; they are half-breeds and mixed breeds. The same applies to other races.

These Mulattoes are regular in their features just like other races and sometimes more impressive in personality. Some of the outstanding men in America and other countries were what they called mulattoes. Such men as Frederick Douglas, Booker T. Washington, Mordecai Johnson and others in America, also General Antonia Maceo, the Cuban Rebel leader, would be classed as a mulatto. They would be a credit to any race—black or white.

Here I would like to be distinctly understood, that I am not advocating amalgamation nor intermarriage among races in America, for that will never happen, but we are defending the Negro blood and trying to prove that it is not inferior. The mixed breeds are not mulattoes nor hybrids, but real men and its pure blooded Negroes are real men and the black race comes down from the ancient days with the richest heritage in history. Our race does not have to mix to rise.

I have critically noticed in my research of various books written by prejudiced authors on the subject of "Anthropology and History," that they often major the text of their comparison in the difference between the black and white races, more than they do all other darker races combined, constantly referring to Negroes as "inferiors," thus measuring the standard of race on the basic theory of evolution, a

[4]

science which achieved its pre-eminence under Charles Darwin and followed by scores of others, which strives to prove that the Negro Race is the link between the missing link of other races and the anthropoid.

This group of scientists describe man as a member of the order of mammals called "Primate" including apes, monkeys, and men, divided into three groups but relatively so with a common ancestral primate, an anthropoid ape of which they claim now extinct the missing link. They further claim that the Negro in Africa was the first to evolve from this ape-like man and thus from the Negro, the Brown, Yellow and White Races evolved in succession.

This theory was also sustained by Camper in his measurement of skulls in which he claims that the Negro is an immediate step between the white race and the Orang (ape), the Orang measures sixty-four degrees, the Negro seventy, the white eighty which places the Negro in measurement only six degrees above that of the ape. Darwin and Camper are worse than ridiculous, for the size of the head has nothing to do with the size of the brain. One man may have a large head but thin grey matter, while the other may have a small head but possess a greater depth of the Sulci and a thicker grey matter. The latter would be far more intelligent than the former with a large head and a thin grey matter. If large heads were the symbols of intelligence, elephants would rule the world. Their heads are large enough but unfortunately, they contain no grey matter, and often used for the seat of his master.

The theory of evolution is built on a false hypothesis. While the argument may carry some biological similarities or some likeness in physical structure between the races of men and apes but scientists have not yet been able to discover one single fact sufficient to defend their claim in all the prospective fields of systematic zoology.

Supplement

Alexander Goldenweise, the scientist in his book *"Early Civilization"* (Pages 5 and 6) says: "There is however no indication that the revealed differences between White and Negro's brains stand for potential inferiority on the part of the Negro."

If there were such a thing as a missing link, where is it? Some claim that the ape-man is now extinct—he died out. Then why not resurrect its skeleton as they have other prehistoric animals.

If they should find such creatures, how could they prove that it was the ancestor of the Adamic Race? Prof. Eugene Dubois claimed to have discovered the missing link, Pithecanthropus man at Wadjak, Java, in 1891, but Dr. Felix Von Lushan, the German scientist, said that Dr. Dubois' discovery turned out to be an oversized ape. And what scientists have been able to reason from the unknown to the known and arrive at an elaborate conclusion? None. If man evolved from an anthropoid Primate, why was it that the ape did not evolve? The same cause upon the same thing in the same climate and environment would have produced the same effect. Man did not come from an evolutionary process. He was created a man from the beginning, the Creator did not have to make a monkey blueprint to make a man and if there is any monkey business, man made that himself, but not his Creator. I have seriously wondered what was the cause of the Science of Evolution and to what purpose could it attain; and why would those who are classed as outstanding scholars burn their midnight oil on such a worthless and frivolous subject. But I soon discovered that the logical tendency of the absurd evolutionists arguments were founded on racial biasness, but I hesitated to commit myself on such criticism however logical my treatise might have been until I had found some anthropologist, who would be an established witness to my claim. After that I found in the volume written by Oscar Perchell, "The Races of Man," pages 6 and 7, in which he says: "As soon as the term (evolution) was invented for the typical varieties of the human race, a dispute arose as to whether the nations of the earth are divisible into different species on only different varieties often as in this instance, it is the highest and most obscure problem which most strangely attracts the inexperienced hurrying to premature and worthless conclusion.

Nor was it even with unprejudiced minds for some tried to harmonize it with the Hebrew Legend of the first human pair, while others strove to establish the plurality of species to withdraw the sympathy from the Negro and to hush the appeal of consciousness, against the degradation of man." I was very much pleased to find that Mr. Oscar Perchell agrees with me and substantiates my contentions that the fundamental cause of the science of evolution was based upon racial prejudice, it is a direct attack upon the black man. Their scientists after finding that the Negro was the first and oldest race, then sought to modernize the background of African History, by asserting that the primitive, or the first man descended from an anthropoid or ape-like man and from this anthropoid descended the Negrito and the Negro who were the first to evolve which was followed in succession of evolution of races, such as the Negritos "Negro" the Australian, the Brown, the Yellow and the White, thus he builds a false hypothesis by saying that each evolving stage produces a new creation and that man became higher in intelligence—that each ascending chain produces a higher breed which mean that the farther away that the breeding gets from the ape, the more human it becomes and thus he makes the Negro the Lower Scale of human society. Such false teaching destroys the doctrine of the Divine Creation and severs the ties of the common Brotherhood of man and impregnates the mind of various nations with a false conception of themselves which already has proven to be destructive to the common welfare of man throughout the world. If the biological science of the brotherhood man's relation to man had been taught and preached among the nations of the earth and if the evolutionist had spent one-third of his interest in teaching the unity of nations rather than trying to prove man's relation to the monkey this world today would have been a far more decent place for human habitation.

I made another survey in my research work, because I was very much concerned about where the evolutionist got the theory of evolving the species to build his hypothesis upon? I discovered that his false argument that the first man sprang from the Anthropoid or Primate something like an ape or the Totemic man with the tale of a Lion, Ape or Zoo type was built from a premise of false legend because the old time Theologian and Anthropologist were ignorant of the Totemic sign language. Totemic sign language has also found its expression in our Bible, in the mythology of Greece and Rome. It bears out an expression, if we only knew its interpretation, such terms as a lion with eagle wings, a leopard with four heads and wings of a fowl, a half woman and half fish, the Egyptian Sphinx with a woman's face and lion's body, or a man with a tail like a lion or an ape. Such terms have no zoological bearing, they are only parables and symbols of a thought conveyed. For further reference of the Totemic man read (Page 436, Vol. I) (Ancient Egypt the Light of the World) by Gerald Massey.

Sir William Dawson says in his book (Meeting Place of Geology and History) (Pages 22-23).

"It may also be objected that if held by some evolutionist man developed from lower animals— even should some animals, either recent or past, he discovered intermediate in structure between man and the highest apes, we should still require proofs that it was the ancestor of man for the occurrence of connecting former or otherwise as the fact stands, the earliest known remains of man are still human and tell us nothing as to previous developments."

As to Negroes and monkeys there is absolutely

no comparison. Other races have far greater similarity to the monkey and ape than the Negro. The Negroes as a race have wooly and curly hair and thick lips, monkeys and apes have straight hair and thin lips.

If wooly hair had been a symbol of inferiority the prophet Daniel and St. John the Seer, of Patmos would not have featured in their prophecies of Jesus Christ, the Messianic King, as having hair like "Lamb's wool" in the likeness of the Black Kings that ruled Empires of the Ancient East. John said that "his feet looked like brass burned in a furnace." Rev. 1 Chapter, 14th and 15th Verses.

And even Buddha, the great founder of the Religion that bears his name has distinctly Negroid features, thick lips—he was a black man.

Jean Finot, in his book (Racial Prejudices) (Page 106-7) says about the Negro "We insist the odd progressing race which demonstrates that in this case evolution and progress go from the yellow and the white races to the Negro, his hair becomes in this way the supreme expression of progress the goal toward which all the hair of other people ought to tend".

Finot says, "If man is more noble as the distance between him and the anthropoid ape widen, it must not be forgotten that these monkeys have straight and little undulated hair resembling that of the yellow races and the American people and perceptibly approaching the Europeans, Berbers and Semites. The wooly hair of the Negro has nothing in common with apes, it procures for them in this way a decided advantage over men of other colors."

[10]

The scientist Alexander Goldenweiser in Book Early Civilization Page 4 says, "The Negro far developed external lips a specially human trait and in this particular the Negro represents 'man physical' more distinctly than any other race."

The true history of the black man as a race for the past five hundred years has been eliminated by many prejudiced writers, who with their high sounding phrases and technical terms—A display of scholarship in vocabulary, rather the basic facts of realities, place the Negro only as a slave from time immemorial as a hewer of wood and drawer of water, while there have been others who took a more liberal view, but even then, they were not definite enough in argument to build up resistance against the school of thought established. But in my research I have been able to find enough reliable data of facts of the Negro's history to give a clear understanding in relinking his past with his present environments.

Ethiopia, Egypt mean black. The word Egypt —the "land of the Blacks", Ethiopia—"Sun burnt faces".

(a) The Garden of Eden in Ethiopia, Africa as the cradle of the human race has been thoroughly established, recent discoveries as well as old have thrown much light upon this subject with little if any conjecture to the BIBLE version of creation.

(b) Dr. Churchward an English anthropologist in his book (Page 11-12) "The Evolution of Primitive Man", says, "From studies I have made during many years, I am fully convinced that the preconceived ideas of many scientists as the origin of the human race as regards to dates and places are erroneous and that the human race did not originate in Asia or any other part of the world, but in Africa".

(c) Moses in his book of Genesis 12:13 refers to Ethiopia. "The second river that went out of Eden is Gishon, that is, it that compasseth the whole land of Ethiopia."

(d) Josephus, the Jewish Historian says, "Gishon ran through Egypt and denotes that it rises in the East which the Greeks called Nile, the River of Ham."

(e) The Book called "Egypt the Light of the World", a translation from the Egyptian Scriptures by Gerald Massey, says "The Egyptian Record when read will tell us plainly that the human birth-place was a land of the Papyms Reed at horn of the earth that is in the equator from where the Sacred River ran to the valley of the Nile with plenty. The Gulf of Aden on the East Coast of Africa is also a traditional name somewhat similar to Eden, the name of Adam's garden."

(f) Black Adam. Alexander Winchell in his book "Preadamites," page 158, says, "There is indeed a legend in existence which has obtained a wide spread currency according to which the first man was dark or black in complexion. There is even said to be a tablet in the British Museum brought by the late George Smith, on which an inscription which lends strange countenance to the legend of the Black Adam." Mark K-3364 British Museum—Preadamites.

(g) The Book titled the "Idigenous Races of the

Earth" by Nott and Gliddon on Page 510 quotes Dr. Volney in saying, "It must be concluded that the process of nature in human species is the transmutation of the characteristic of the Negro into the European or the evolution of white varieties in the black races of men which leads us to the inference that the Primitive stock of men were negroes which has every appearance of truth—on the whole there are reasons which leads us to adopt the conclusion that the primitive stock of men were probably Negroes. I know no argument to set on the other side."

(h) Colonel A. Brighane in his volume "The Shadow of the Atlantis," page 206, quotes Dr. A. Herrman, the German Scientist in his research who says "Come to the conclusion of the mysterious River Gishon was nothing else than the Nile and that therefore the site of Eden should be sought in Abyssinia" (Ethiopia).

(i) Prof. Jerome Dowd in his volume Negro Races vol. 3, page 288 says: "The connection between the Palaeolithic man and the Negro is very apparent. The African Negro seems to be the survival of the first inhabitant of the earth, the Palaeolithic man who remain in Africa may have there developed a black skin and wooly hair while those migrating North and East may have developed in transit the Caucasian and Mongolian that the white man originated in Africa, it is now generally conceded."

Brighane says: Shadow of Atlantis, page 229, "All this material proves that at one time the black continent was the home of comparatively elevated cul-

ture and Prof. Frobenius supposes that some regions of Northern-Western and Northern Africa at
one time were subjected to mighty cultural influ-
ences in fact my personal interview of collaborator
of Frobenius. Professor Obermayer, I was able to
glean that Prof. Frobenius is inclined to seek the
cradle of the human culture in Africa instead of
Asia and to derive a prehistoric culture from the
mysterious race which once populated the fertile
region of the Sahara."

2

Prehistoric Ethiopia or the Empire of the Atlantis

The Ancient Empire of Ethiopia comes down to us from a very remote Past—from the Ancient of days with the richest heritage in history. Ethiopia was considered by the Greeks to be the home of the Gods and retreat of the Muses. A land of fertile fields, with river beds of diamonds with mountains of gold and "Isles of the Blessed". The land of the setting sun where the giant Atlas was compelled by the Olympian Jove to prop up the heaven upon his head and shoulders.

The vast desert which lies south of the Atlas known as the Sahara is called by the Moors "The Garden of Allah" where the chariot of the Gods whose flaming wheels burnt the soil into sands, scorched the children of Africa and crisped their hair for which the word Ethiopia is termed, "Sun burnt by the Gods". The word Ethiopia was originally pronounced Aethiopia meaning "sun-burnt faces".

Pliny, the Roman Historian says that the original Ethiopia was called Aetheria or Aeria which derived its name from Aether, the Son of the God Vulcan which means heat (Vulcanised). Pliny says that "the whole country of Africa was called Aetheria or Aeria and later Atlantia".

The Greek writer concluded the term Atheria to mean Ethiopia while another Roman writer Aulus Cellus used the term Aeria for both Africa and Crete—the Roman converted the term Aeria to the name Africa. Many renown men in Roman history who had performed heroic deeds in Africa were often surnamed "Africanus". But according to tradition the wife of the giant Atlas was called Atheria. Tradition speaks of Atlas as a great King and the founder of the Atlantean Empire whose vast realm ruled over two-thirds of the earth—including Africa, Asia, Europe, Mexico, Central and South America.

Both Ancient and modern writers, and tradition, place Ethiopia in Atlantis. The term Atlantis was the name of a continent or portion of Africa according to Greek mythology and the Ancient Egyptian records.

The scientist Leo Frobenius says: "That the Atlantis was a part of Nigeria (West Africa) in the Yaruba country and the African Atlantis was the fragment survival".

Colonel A. Brighane in his book *The Shadow of the Atlantis*, page 214, says, "Other Ancient authors are even more specific and identify Ethiopia with Atlantis—The above facts lead to the conclusion that in antiquity the name Ethiopia was given to a region of the Atlantis, this region was peopled by a dark skinned people and a fine climate". We

[16]

have shown in the foregoing paragraphs that the term Atlantis and Ethiopia relates to the same country and people.

James Braunwell in his book *Atlantis*, Page 107, says: "Modern theory has eight main hypothesis that Atlantis was America and North Africa and Nigeria". He further states that they became a race four or five million years ago and were mahogany black in color, Page 198.

Mr. George Smith, in the *Chaldean Account of Creation*, Page 78, deciphered from the Babylonian tablet that there was an original race of men at the beginning of the Chaldean history, a dark race who were called Ad-Mi or Ad-Ami the people of Ad or Atlantis.

Mr. Alexander Winchell, in his book *Pre-Adamites,* tries to make it appear that there were two Adams, a black one and a white one; but he utterly fails in his argument and with the most striking evidence he affirms the very fact of which he strives to deny when he refers in his finding the tablet of a *Black Adam*. In his volume he says: "There is indeed a legend which has attained wide-spread currency, according to which the first man was of dark complexion. As I am about to argue some black races first represented humanity upon the earth," so far as Mr. Winchell's Pre-Adamites, there were no such beings. There was but one Adam or the first man and all the others were Junior Adams.

It is logical to believe that man was created and lived for a time in a very primitive state. The Bible tells us that the first pair were "naked" and, becoming ashamed of themselves, they pinned "fig leaves" to hide their nakedness. It is said according to the Mosaic version that Adam lived to be nine hundred and thirty years of age—whether this period was authentic or Dogmatic, it is not mine to discuss, neither do I question the chronology of the Bible but I am dealing with the facts of history as they present themselves. I do not build the hypothesis of my argument upon the longevity of Adam's life with the comparison of the present limit of man's three score and ten years on earth with the ten years of Grace—which makes eighty years, which is a vast difference to nine hundred and thirty of Adams existence.

But I do claim that the name Adam became a symbol for Divinity, King, Nationality and Religion for many centuries in the Ancient past and even names of many places such as towns. According to tradition Adam was the world's first Patriarch and King, if he lived nine hundred and thirty years he lived long enough to build a nation and to become a King. He was the first whom God gave . . . "Dominion over the fish of the Sea and over the fowls of the Air, and over the cattle, and over all the earth and over every creeping thing that creepeth upon the earth." Genesis 1:26.

In Smith's *Sacred Annals*, Page 49, he quotes the Hebrew commentator as saying: "Our Rabbis assert that Adam Our Father of blessed memory composed a book of precepts which was delivered by God in Paradise".

Ancient records now in possession of King Halie Selassie say that Aran the thirty-fifth Son of Adam

Son of the "Conquering Lion," Prince Makonnen, Ready for Battle

When Haile Selassie Visited King George V of England in 1925. He Was Known as Ras Tafari, then Prince Regent of Ethiopia and Made a Diplomatic Visit to London. Notice His Wooly Hair Which Clearly Portrays the Identity of His Race

was the first King of Ethiopia. This gives evidence that the first King of Ethiopia was Aran or Ori the thirty-fifth Son of Adam. Josephus, *History of the Jews*—Page 48 (William Whiston, translation) says: "That there is an old tradition which says that Adam was the father of thirty-three sons and twenty-three daughters".

It is a fact beyond all reasonable doubt that there was an Adamic Empire and it produced a culture that comes down to us, and even today, we have not been able to excell and in many respects we have not even equaled. From these we received our alphabet, our culture and our religion.

Donnelley in his *Atlantis,* page 2, tells of the Phoenician Alphabet the parent of the European alphabet derived from the Atlantis alphabet which was also conveyed to Mayo-Central America. It must be remembered that during this remote period South America, Africa and other continents were connected with land bridges, in a practical sense the whole earth was one plot of land. The "Plantation of God" the ocean, had not yet separated them into Continents. This was before ". . . the seas in order stood or earth received her frame."

Nearly all traditional names which begin with "A" comes down to us from far distant periods— Atlantis. These Atlanteans reached the highest culture that has ever been attained by man. The book of Job the oldest book in our Bible and the book of Enoch were written at this period. They had hot and cold water both. They were a great religious people, they gave us our calendar to regulate time. They also had airships, they harnessed the power of gravitation to propell their airships. It is said "Their airships could only fly a few hundred feet above the ground." *Lost Atlantis,* Page 197, James Bramwell.

The doctrine of the Son of God, the basic foundation of Christianity comes from them. They had twelve Patriarch from Adam to Noah. They gave us the number twelve for a formula for our culture. There are twelve signs of the Zodiac, there are twelve hours in a day and twelve months in a year, the twelve Patriarch, the twelve tribes of Israel, twelve apostles and St. John in his book "Revelation" speaks of the twelve gates of new Jerusalem, and twelve foundations of the Holy City.

The very foundation of our language comes down to us from the Atlanean period which was Adamic in its origin, and Moses says: Genesis 2:20, "And Adam named all the cattle, the fowls of the air, and every beast of the field"; Genesis 2:1, "The whole earth was of one language and one speech."

The Ancient names of continents, places, countries, nations, seas, gulfs, oceans and mountain chains begins with "A" which gives us a striking evidence that the whole earth was one language and one speech.

The Africian Language

The Africian Language is the oldest language in the world, had its birth, growth and development beyond the Flood. The language that we call Hebrew is nothing but deviation of the Africian tongue. R. G. Latham in his book *Man and His Migration* Page 156-7 (Ethiopia says: "In the language of Abyssinia the Gheez and Tigre admitted as long as they have been known at all to be Semitic, graduate through Amharic, the Falasha, the Harargi; the Gafat and other languages which may be well studied in Dr. Beke's valuable comparative tablet into the Agon tongue unequivocally, indigenous to Abyssinia", and through this into the true Negro classes but unequivocally as may be the Semitic elements of the Becher, Coptic and Galla their affinities with the tongues of Western and Southern Africa are more so. I weigh my words when I say not equally but more so, changing the expression for every foot in advance, which can be made toward the Semitic tongues in one direction, the Philogist can go a yard toward the Negro ones in the other."

Mr. Latham continues when he says on page 260: "That uniformity of language throughout Africa is greater than in Asia or Europe; is a statement which I have not the hesitation of committing myself. The conviction is that the Semitic tongues are simply African and that all the theories suggested by the term Indo-European must be abandoned or modified."

All the nations of the Ancient East recognized Adam as their common ancestor. In Egypt Adam is called Atem; in Babylonian he is called Admu, in Persian he is called Ada-Mah, in Sanscrit he is called Adim, "the first man," in Hindu is called Adima, and his wife Heva; the Phoenicians worshipped him as a God and called him Adon, the Ancient Greeks recognized him as one of their Chief Dieties and called him Ad-ones. The letter "A" holds the first place in English, Greek and

Hebrew alphabet, such as "A" in English, Alpha in Greek and Aleph in Hebrew. The new year in Ancient times began with April instead of January, such traditional and historic names that begin with "A" more or less came from the Prehistoric period of the Atlantis, such as Aethiopia, Africa, Atlas, Atlantic, Arctic, Ant-Arctic, Amon, Allah, Asia, Arabia, Assyria, Alps, Aryan, Athens, Australia, Aleutians, Alaska, Allegheny, Appalachin, Aztec, Andes, Amazon.

After making my survey of these traditional and historic names throughout the world, to satisfy my curiosity, I made some research in Indian Legends or the Folklore of the American Indian to find whether these names beginning with "A" in America, had anything in common with the meaning of such names beginning with "A" in Africa and other continents of the old world and I soon found that these interpretations are somewhat similar in meaning. The word Alaska, an Indian word for "mainland"; the word Allegheny, an Indian word for "best or first mountain"; the word Appalachian, an Indian word for "people on the other side"; the word Aliquippa, "the Queen of the Delawares" or "First Lady". The traditional names will substantiate the fact that there were one nation, one language, one speech and even today the capital of modern Ethiopian Empire is called "Addis Ababa", the Chief City. There were once one language, the different language and dialects of the various races and nations show a kindred relation in their speech.

Universal Alphabet

In Use Many Thousands Years Before the Flood.

		African		American	
		No. 1.	2.	3.	
Ear	AIPS.	A.			A.
Eye.	ESH.	E.			EI.
Nose.	IFR.	I.			IZ.
Tongue.	OMBR.	O.			OW.
Hand.	VULD.	U.			UW.
Earth.	LAMBD.	L.			IL.
Sea.	MAH.	M.			IM.
Air.	NISP.	N.			IN.
Fire	RASH.	P.			IR.
Sun.	BAP.	B p.			IB.
Moon.	CEK.	C. k.			UK.
Mars.	DOR.	D. t.			ID ET
Mer'y	GOREG.	G.			IGH.
Venus.	UAF.	V. f.			UW.
Saturn.	SIASH.	S. sh			ES. ISH.
Jup'r	THEUE	Thz.			UZ.

Josiah Priest in his book: "American Antiquities," page 117, says: "Under the Figures 1 and 2 are the African or Lybian Characters, the primitive letters of the most ancient nations of Africa. Under Figure 3 are the American letters, or letter of Otolum, an ancient city, the ruins of which is found in South America. The similarity, which appears between the African letters and the letters of America, if not exact, shows beyond a doubt that these two nations used languages known in Lybia or Africa, as well as in America."

I had always believed that the Atlantes of Africa have partly colonized America. Page 119, "American Antiquities."

[23]

Who They Were, The Atlanteans?

The Great Ethiopian or Cushite which in the earliest ages prevailed as Mr. Rawlinson says: "From the Caucaus mountains to the Indian Ocean from the shores of the Mediterranean to the mouth of the Ganges" *Atlantis,* Page 278. Mr. Rawlinson here fails to mention that the seat of the Atlantean Empire was in Africa. But he admitted the fact the Atlanteans were an Ethiopian or Cushite Nation. Donnelly also quotes *Atlantis,* Page 452-3, Baldwin's *Prehistoric Nations,* Page 114, "The Cushite Nation was the successors of the Atlantean whose very Ancient Empire extended from Spain to Syria were first to establish independent municipal Republics with the right to govern themselves. This system of government was perpetuated through Phenicia, African Berber, Hindu, middle ages in Europe and the United States".

Baldwin strives to make it appear that the seat of the Atlantean Power was in Spain, but Mr. Baldwin tells us that the Atlanteans were Cushites and since they were Cushites they belong to the Black Race and the seat of this Great Empire was in Ethiopia. The Cushite or Ethiopian Empire known as the Atlantis ruled and governed the entire habitable earth, such continents as Asia, Europe and South America also the southern portion of North America was under their sway.

Dr. F. Freeman quoting Rollins in his volume *Yaradee, Plea for Africa,* Page 34, says: "The Cushites or Ethiopian established the first regular policy which history records. The first great city described in history was built by them, they surrounded it with walls which according to Rallin, were eighty-seven feet in thickness, three hundred and fifty furlongs in circumference." And even this stupendous work they shortly after eclipsed by another of which Diodorus says: "Never did any city come up to the greatness and magnificance of this, Pyramids, Obelisk and Mausoleum still stand as if in mockery of the very cruelty of man, a memorial of that daring enterprise and skill which made Egypt, the mother of Science and for a time, the mistress of the world. It is a fact well attested by history that Ethiopia once bore sway not only in Africa, but over almost all Asia and it is said that even two continents could not afford field for the expansion of their energies. They found their way into Europe, and made the settlement on the Western Coast of Spain, called from them "Iberian Ethiopia" and says a distinguished writer, "Wherever they went, they were rewarded for their wisdom". That very light which long since blazed before the world in Greece and Rome and which now rises to its noon-day splendor under the auspices of Christianity, in Europe and America, be it remembered, my dear children, was kindled on the dark shores of Africa. When I think of these things, my spirit stirs within me, and I am almost impatient to see that light reflected back on Africa again. Yes, the light of science combined with the glorious light of the Gospel of Christ."

The Scientist Volney said during the period of American Slavery: "How are we astonished when we reflect that to the Race of Negroes, at present our slaves, and the object of our extreme contempt we owe our arts and science and even the very use of Speech." *Yaradee-Plea for Africa*, Page 28.

Who were the Ethiopian or Cushite People?

The Ethiopian the *Jewish encyclopedia*, Page 258-Vol. 5, says: "The Ethiopians (dusky face) cover all nation of Eastern or Central Africa but designated as Ethiopian proper the Nile Valley from Syrene to Khatoum the inhabitants of their country were more or less pure Negroes."

The Cushite

The *Jewish encyclopedia*, Vol. 4, Page 395, "The Talmudic application of the name such as 'Cush' black person of the Negro Race distinguished by their color from other men". We have prominent authors who corroborate the above facts that Ethiopian and Negroes mean one and the same race.

Brighane in his book *Shadow of Atlantis*, Page 215, says: "For a certain time these Ethiopians inhabited the mountain Atlas regions and from there migrated to Abyssinia which they name in rememberance of their father land (Atlantis) these dark skinned new comers were cultured more so than Aborigines of Egypt."

Pritchard—*Natural History of Man*, Page 120, says: "The African Negroes derived from the Southern face of the Mount Atlas; they are, however, named simply Ethiopian Race from the Ethiopians who were the only black people known to the Ancients in very remote period". But farther on Mr. Pritchard is more explicit on Page 278,

[26]

when he says: "The Abyssinians are recorded among the black races".

Dr. Edward W. Blyden, a prominent Negro author, historian and oriental scholar says in his volume, *The Negro in Ancient History* in which he quotes an article from the *Princeston Review* says: "The Ethiopian Race from whom the modern Negro or African descended can claim as earlier history, with the exception of the Jews, to any living people on the face of the earth. History as well as monumental discoveries give them a place in history as far back as Egypt, if not farther."

The Ethiopian or African Race though they have long lost the civilization which once existed on the upper Nile, have increased and multiplied until they are now with the exception of the Chinese, the largest single human family of the ea..h. They have extended themselves in every direction over that Great continent of Africa from the Southern border of the Sahara to the Cape of Good Hope".

Paul Radin in his book *Racial Myth,* Page 17 says: "The Ancestors of the Negro in their primary period of human culture would mean that Negroes have been in contact with civilization for thirty thousand years, a fact correlated with the existence of numerous stations of the old Stone Age civilization along the whole coast of East Africa to the Cape". Mr. Radin continues on Page 55, in the same volume places the Negro existence on earth, to one hundred thousand years when he says: "The old Stone Age beginning one hundred thousand years ago, we cannot make out any good case for any one of our present Races. If a case can be made for one of the present is for the Negro. For the white race, all we can say or hope that they are in some degree, descended from the Cro-Magnon Race which flourished in Europe twenty-five thousand years ago."

A press dispatch from London, May 27th, to the *Christian Science Monitor,* tells of a recent discovery in Kenya, East Africa by Dr. L. S. Leakey and his wife, which has aroused great interest among Archeologists, where they found a "considerable number of Prehistoric Stone implements, and also the existence of a cultured people in East Africa so far found only in the middle Pleistocene age which dates back some hundred of thousand years"

History Beyond History

After you have read the last page of the dusky manuscript of the most ancient texts and have deciphered the language of the Hieroglyphics on the base of the Ethiopian and Egyptian Pyramid and gazed at the negroid features of the Sphinx in the Delta of the Nile and excavated the hoary tombs of the Ethiopian and Egyptian Pharoahs that sleep in the Valley of Luxor, you must admit these were achievements wrought by the Black Sons of Ethiopia whom modern history falsely classifies as some other race. But when you have fully examined ancient records of Egypt and Ethiopia on tombs and monuments, the Archaeologist will carry you many thousand years farther back than the history written in books of Stone, to a culture which had its beginning in the Old Stone Age, when the Negro lighted the torch of civilization many thousand years ago.

History Resting on Monuments

A monument is history recorded on Stone and a photograph chisled or sculptured on polish marble features the likeness of the people who erected it. This being true it gives license to say that without a shadow of doubt, a monument is more reliable than history and tells a truth more real than tradition and demonstrates a fact that is "stranger than fiction". The Historian Hereen says: "A monument bears witness of a fact more clearly and certain than could be done by the statement of a writer. The fact that the people who erected this monument had attained a degree of civilization without which they could not have erected it".

The Ancient monuments and Statues of Ancient Kings and Gods through Africa, Asia and America feature the Negro Race. The Sphinx in Egypt and Ethiopia is decidedly Negroid features and also the Statue of Budha in India and the East, and the statue of a gigantic Negro's features on the Ancient monuments near the Mexican Volcano of Taxila, Mexico and the statue of the Indian Gods in Central America and the Archaeologist collection of Negro Statues in Quita, Ecuador, South America. According to a reliable archaeologist Colonel E. Brighane, *Shadows of Atlantis*, page 40, who says "The Negro has been in America at least twenty thousand years." Black men built the massive pyramid on the Banks of the Nile whose lofty structure reach the clouds and made Egypt a wilderness of architectural wonder. Broughton—*Ancient People,* Pages 88-9: "The Great Pyramid that was built during the 4th Dynasty by King 'Khufu' the foursided

Pyramids measured seven hundred and fifty-six feet, covered thirteen acres of land. This stupendous mass of stone rose to the height of four hundred and eighty feet above its base, thirty feet higher than Saint Peters at Rome. One hundred and twenty feet higher than Saint Paul's in London and exceeded the capitol at Washington nearly two hundred feet. It is said that the stones contained in this Great Pyramid if they were laid in line of cubic squares would girdle nearly two-thirds of the earth's circumference at the equator."

In Thebes, Luxor, Memphis and Ancient Jerusalem in the days of Melchizedek and even Babylon, Ninevah and Tyre were the products of Ethiopian culture. The hanging gardens and swinging palaces of Babylon were reckoned among the seven wonders of the world. The magnificent cities of the Empire of the Ancient East, now gone with the wind, their ancient sites though heaped in ruins remain an object of study to the modern archaeologist.

The Historian Hereen says: "From the remote times to the present, one of the most celebrated and yet most mysterious nations was Ethiopia. In the early tradition of nearly all civilized nations the name of this distant people is found.

"They are the remotest nation, the most just of men, the favorite of the Gods and when the faint gleam of tradition and fables gives way to clear light of history, the lustre of the Ethiopian is not diminished, they still continue as the object of curiosity and admiration; the pen of cautious, clear sighted historian often paint them in the highest rank of knowledge and civilization."

The Black Christ or the Second Adam

The very foundation of our Christian Doctrine and faith was erected upon the culture which came down through the ages from the Atlantean civilization, also our system of Government and Religion.

Many devout souls like Enoch and Job walked and talked with God and their souls were translated to the realm of eternal bliss—in the peaceful abode of Amenta (Paradise) where they were purified and their spirits were presented blameless before the throne of the God Amon (Amen).

The word Amon or "Amen" comes down to us today. The word Amon or Amen originally were the Egyptian and Ethiopian words for God. The doctrine of Divine duality was based upon the Egyptian Pharaoh as the Father and the heir apparent as the Son—the ever coming King in the person of the Prince who was always born to be King. The Father was the King of Egypt and the Son was the Prince of Ethiopia which was the birth-place in an earlier time and remained the typical birth-place for the young Prince for all time.

Messu was the Root of the Messiah by nature and by name. The Prince of Ethiopia is the Messu . . .

The Lord's anointed is called the Messiah in Hebrew, Kristu in Greek; Chrestus in Latin and is Messu in Egyptian, Messu signifies the son or heir apparent, the Prince of Ethiopia. Gerald Massey *Ancient Egypt in the Light of the World.* Page 521, Vol. 1.

The Doctrine of the coming Messiah, Jesus Christ as the Son of God, did not originate with the Jews in Palestine but with the Ancient Ethiopians who came down from the last Atlantean culture. The Pharaohs of Egypt were more or less selected from the Priests and many of them were very religious. Some of them would baptize their soldiers before going into battle. The most of these Pharaoh took their wives from Ethiopia because Ethiopia was to them the Holy Land where once dwelt the happy pair Adam and Eve. An Egyptian Pharaoh who married an Ethiopian wife looked forward to the time that a crown Prince would be born who would become the second Adam and would restore the lost paradise and universal brotherhood among the nations of the earth.

You find in the History of the 18th Dynasty of Egypt the marriage of King Ahames to Queen Neferti of Ethiopia. Queen Neferti was the spiritual wife of the God Amon. There were many young Princesses of the royal house of Ethiopia who dedicated their lives to become the spiritual wives of the God Amon (Amen), but the system was different from that of a Catholic Nun. The custom of being the spiritual wife Amon did not destroy their rights or privilege to marry but the sons born to this union went in the name of the spiritual husband instead of the real father. I am told in some parts of Africa today the children go in the name of their mothers. You will notice in this history of Ahames and Queen Neferti, that their first son was named Amoniphis, the 1st, there were four Kings of the 18th Dynasty known as Amoniphis, which came in succession to the throne. The Sons of God referred to in our Bible in the book of

Genesis does not mean that they were spiritual beings as some Theologian would term them but they were Princes, Kings or men of Royal blood.

Moses married an Ethiopian Princess whose father Jethro, was a Priest-King while some Jewish Talmudic writers say that Moses wife was a woman of Ethiopia. The Jews as a nation took the idea of their Religion from the Egyptian who in turn got theirs from Ethiopia, the mother country of Egypt.

All the nations of the Ancient East looked for a second Adam. They expected him to come from Ethiopia or of an Ethiopian lineage. David in his book of Psalms 87:4 says "I make mention of Rahab and Babylon to them that know me; behold Philistia and Tyre with Ethiopia; this man was born there". Daniel 7:9 speaks of him as "the Ancient of Days and the hair on his head was like pure wool".

The coming of the Messu the Messiah as a colonial God was believed by the Greeks during the period when Homer sung his Illiad he says:

"Jove to the Solemn Banquet gone,
  Beyond the sea, on Ethiopia's shore;
  He thought it *not* disdain to grace,
  And dined with Ethiopia's blameless Race."

Whether in the name Jehovah, Jupiter, Jove or Jesus the nations of the Ancient expected the coming Messiah.

The Ethiopian Line of Christ, the Ancestors of Jesus Christ were of the Ethiopian Race—according to Josephus, which says: "That Canaan the fourth

[33]

Son of Ham inhabited the country now called Judea and called it from his name Canaan and that Ragmus the Son of Canaan had two sons, one of which was Judadas and his descendants were called Judadean a nation of Western Ethiopians. The name, Judadean in short the term, is Judeans or Jews. The Hamite and Semites were one and the same people the Jews were a direct branch of the Ethiopian Race. King Solomon was a Black man, he was the Son of David by a Canaanitish woman. He speaks of himself in the songs of Solomon: "I am black, but comely, O ye daughter of Jerusalem," Look not upon me because I am black, because the Sun hath both looked upon me" (Songs of Solomon 5:6).

From the direct lineage of David comes the Ancient of Days, the Christ, the Second Adam.

This Atlantean system of Government with its vast realm of States stretched to the far corners of the earth. Each State remained its separate unit but existed as a subordinate power, like the States in our Union. But in the Atlantean States, subordinate rulers bore the title of Kings instead of Governor and the Chief Ruler bore the title of "King of Kings." This system of Government is still practiced in Ethiopia that is why Haile Selassie is called "King of Kings." Ethiopia today is only a fragmental survival of the old Atlantean culture.

Christian ideals are built on the culture of the Atlantis, a culture which has ever worked and toiled and longed for the restoration of the Lost Paradise. It has been the dream of prophets, Statesmen and Kings, Wilsons "League of Nations," Willkie's

[34]

Ras Kassa, the Supreme Commander of the Ethiopian Forces on the Border Section, and a Master Strategist

"One World," Roosevelt-Churchill's Atlantic Charter. These men may have had some selfish objective, yet deep in their hearts, souls and minds they look for a better world wherein dwelleth Righteousness and Peace. The world most anxiously awaits the coming of the Messiah, the Christ which is the Second Adam: when

> Jesus shall reign wherever Sun;
> Doth his successive journey run;
> His Empire stretch from shore to shore
> Till moon shall wane and wax no more;
> From north to south the princes meet
> And pay their homage at his feet,
> And Western Empires own my Lord,
> And Savage tribes attend His word.

3

The Ethiopian Empire

The Empire of Ethiopia as a whole may be divided into three distinct periods, at least we take the occasion to do so for the convenience of its history.

The Adamic Period, is the one that is briefly described in Chapter 2 under title, "Prehistoric Ethiopia or the Empire of the Atlantis."

Ethiopian Chronologist says that Aram os Ori, the thirty-fifth Son of Adam ascended the throne of Ethiopia in the year of the world 970; Before Christ, 4470 years, and that twenty-one Kings had ascended the throne before the Flood, but there is another record of the long list of Kings, according to Ethiopian Historians, that was probably more accurate than this, but was carried to Egypt when the Ethiopian Kings ruled that country, and was destroyed when her power was overthrown.

The Ethiopians, as I have already stated, were the founders of the Egyptian Empire and were the most powerful people of the Ancient World.

Braughton's HISTORY OF ANCIENT PEOPLE (Page 31) says, "According to progressive theory, the earth may have been first peopled by men black in color, if so, the Blacks reached their cultural climax in Ancient times, however, how much Egypt, India and Southern Europe owe to them may never be known." He further states on (Page 31) "Of the fifteen thousand years of the world existence, nine thousand were spent under Black Domination."

The Atlantean Empire (Ad lanteen) or the Adamic Dynasty, lasted until the Flood and was succeeded by the Hamitic Period.

The Dynasty of Ham

This Dynasty had its beginning about 2,635 years B.C. The direct line of the Hamitic Dynasty lasted 650 years and twenty-five Kings are said to have reigned in succession during that period. While it is said that Ham was the Ancestor of the Black Race, this is true only in the same sense that George Washington was the "Father of His Country"; this does not make Washington the Ancestor of the White Americans, although Washington was a white man. Ham was not the father of the Black Race, the Bible does not say so, but Ham was a Black King and father of his country. The Black Race had a background of twenty-five thousand years of culture before Ham ascended the throne,—this is according to Prehistoric records, dating back to the Old Stone Age. So did the name, "Cush," the Son of Ham, become a symbol of Nationality and has been converted to mean Ethiopia or Negro, but he also was a great King in those remote times. It appears that King Ham's reign was more or less confined to the continent of Africa, as the scripture

[37]

refers to Africa as the "Land of Ham," but the Kushite Empire seemed to have held its sway in Africa, and extended its sway over the Greater part of Asia.

Josepehus's HISTORY OF THE JEWS (Book 1, Page 56) (William Whiston translation) speaks of Cush as a King when he says, "Time has not hurt the name of Cush for the Ethiopians over whom he reigned are even to this day both by themselves and all men in Asia, called Cushites."

The Hindo-Kush mountain in Asia derived its traditional name from King Cush. The term Kush means Black Nation, but the Ancient writers differentiated the name between the King and the people. The Ethiopian or Cushite Kings were called "The Royal Son of Kush" and his Black subjects Cushites—the King was looked on as the "Father of his Country."

The most outstanding Dynasties of the Egyptian Empire were 12th, 18th, 19th and 25th, which were almost Ethiopian or Cushite reign exclusive.

H. R. Hall's ANCIENT HISTORY OF THE NEAR EAST (Page 271) says, "All we know of the Kushites (Cushites) of the 12th Dynasty were Negroes and the 18th Dynasty from the latter period Kush was in full and peaceful control of the Egyptians."

King Nimrod, the Royal Son Cush, the founder of the Babylonian Empire, built the City of Babylon and Nineveh, whose hanging gardens and swinging palaces were reckoned among the Seven Wonders of the World.

The last and one of the most prominent rulers

[38]

of the Hamitic Dynasty, was known as Makeda, the Queen of Sheba in the Bible; this venerated queen was the Royal Guest at the temple and palace of King Solomon. She came with a long, brilliant train of followers, bringing gifts and tribute to the Jewish King. Ethiopian History and reliable tradition say that the Queen of Sheba became the mother of a child by Solomon whom she named Menelik, which meant "The Son of a Wise Man." It is said when the Prince was 18 years old, his mother sent him to his father to be educated at Jerusalem and to have the influence and training of his wise father.

It is said that Prince Menelik became so much inspired by his father's system of government that he stole the Ark of the Covenant, which contained the Ten Commandments and carried them to Ethiopia.

The House of Solomon

Menelik the first, the Son of the Queen of Sheba, marked the beginning of the Judean Line or the House of Solomon, which had ruled the Nation for more than three thousand years.

I would like to state here frankly that King Solomon's line does not change the Race or Nationality of the Ethiopian Kings as some writers have tried to make it appear, when they speak of the Jewish features of King Selassie, but King Solomon was a Black man, and his mother was a Cananite woman, an Asiatic Ethiopian.

In the Songs of Solomon, Chapter 1, verses 5 and 6, Solomon says, "I am black but commonly. Look not upon me because I am black, because the Sun has looked upon me."

[39]

It is said that King Menelik first introduced the Jewish Religion in Ethiopia, and that the original Ark of the Covenant still remains in the Ethiopian Church at Axum, the Ancient Capital of Ethiopia in the days of the Queen of Sheba.

Ethiopia remained a powerful state, after losing its prestige of a Great Empire up to the period of the Middle Ages, when it was divided into several Semi-independent states governed by a feudal system, although the strifes existing between the powerful Rasses often caused civil and eternal conflict.

These conditions and her struggle for existence and independence from the outside world seriously affected the progress of Ethiopia. She repelled the Mohammedan invasion with only the aid of five hundred Portuguese soldiers. She was later overrun by the war-like Galla tribes from the South, and under the leadership of her noble King, his Majesty's Amada Zion defeated the mighty War Lords of the Kingdom Adel, a Negro State of Arabian culture in East Africa. During the Middle Ages, she fought against the incroachment of both Mohammedans and Pagans alike, but during the later years in Ethiopian History, she has had to battle with overwhelming odds against the so-called Christian Powers who were a more formable foe, and who had bigger and better guns and more destructive engines of war, and were by far more brutal and ruthless in their attacks. This has much to do with the handicaps which have constantly encountered its people through the centuries, but she was and is still the Lion of God and she has been able to survive the shock of fifty centuries, after the fall of the old Atlantean Empire, which existed many thousand years before the Flood. During the Dark Ages, she slept in the bed of a Feudal State and had her first real awakening under the leadership of King Theodore, a man of extraordinary character. He was born a poor boy and was supposed to be the nephew of a small Chieftain. Theodore, as a young man, organized a small party of men, seized large tracts of territory, defeated the Egyptian attack on the country, conquered his father-in-law in battle, and overrun the rest of the country. He then captured the son of Haile Milikot, Sehala Mariam, who was afterwards known as Menelik the II, and Theodore's Government was soon reorganized by Great Britain and other Powers.

Theodore was indeed a great King—in fact he made himself a King by his own fierceless achievements; however, the latter part of his reign was met with a gloomy defeat in war with Great Britain. It is said that Theodore sent an ambassador to the Court of St. James and that Queen Victoria refused to recognize him, and Theodore retaliated by imprisoning the British missionaries in Ethiopia.

The British Government sent out an expedition under the command of Lord Napier and the British encountered the Ethiopians in battle at the strong fortress of Magdala. This battle resulted in the defeat of the Ethiopians, and King Theodore committed suicide after the release of the missionaries. The British troops made no further advances.

The army officials took King Theodore's son, Crown Prince Alamayou, age 7, and brought him to England to Queen Victoria. At the age of 16, the

Prince was sent to India to be educated and trained in Eastern custom and tradition, and later he returned to England to take a post-graduate course in a British University. The Prince returned to England in 1871, and died of pneumonia in Leeds, England, on Nov. 14, 1879. Queen Victoria ordered his burial to be in Windsor Chapel.

King Theodore was succeeded by King John, but his reign was brief; he proclaimed himself as King of Shoa and Gojan, but he was soon killed in battle while fighting the Dervishes.

He was succeeded by Menelik the second, who was the greatest Ethiopian King since the days of Taharqua. Menelik ascended the throne of Ethiopia with drawn sword. The former King John had made a Treaty with Italy, known as the Treaty of Ucciali, which had given Italy the right of protectorate over Ethiopia, but Menelik balked at this agreement and war was declared.

The far-famed Battle of Adorwa decided the issue and the Italian Army met with a disastrous defeat. Menelik then united the Province of Ethiopia into a consolidated Empire and he became the Bismarck of Africa, and European powers looked upon this victory with much concern.

Menelik was succeeded by his grandson, Liu Yassu. We shall deal with Liu Yassu's notorious reign as Regent Ruler, his Mohammedan influence and Pan-African dream in Chapter 10.

The National Church

Judeanism was introduced into Ethiopia by King Solomon's son, Menelik I.

Christianity was carried there by the Ethiopian Eunuch, who was converted and baptized by Saint Phillip, who met the Ethiopian Nobleman while returning from Jerusalem where he had gone to worship. The Ethiopians still retain a Christian Church in Jerusalem. Some writers claim that the Gospel was carried to Ethiopia by Saint Matthew, the Apostle.

During the fourth century after Christ, Ethiopia accepted Christianity as a national religion and her Kings became the defenders of the faith.

Freementius, the first Bishop was consecrated by Athanasius, the African Patriarch of Alexandria, Egypt. The National Church of Ethiopia is Orthodox Catholic, the same as that of Greece. The Bible was first translated into the Ethiopian language (500 A.D.). There are eighty-one books in their Bible, 46 books in the Old Testament and 35 Books in the New Testament. The pictures of the Virgin Mary, the Infant Savior, John the Baptist, and the angels are painted black with wooly hair.

The Ethiopian doctrine of Christ during the early stage of Christianity in 450 A.D. was condemned by the Council of Chalcedon; because the Ethiopian believed only in the one nature of Christ, they rejected the Doctrine that he was both God and man. This Doctrine was looked upon as Heresy and was not accepted by the church at Alexander, but this controversy was settled by the good influence of Ethiopia's noblest Saint, King Tekla

Hamout, who agreed to modify the Doctrine of Ethiopia in accordance with the Coptic Church of Egypt and Greece in order to connect the fellowship of Ethiopia with the Orthodox Churches of the World.

Ethiopia today is a Christian Nation and His Majesty, Haile Selassie, is the defender of the faith, the elect of God and the power of the Trinity.

4

The Ethiopian Pharaoh's Domination of Egypt

In the foregoing chapter we believe we have satisfactorily proven that the Ancient Egyptian were an Ethiopian Race and that their greatest Rulers were more or less of the Ethiopian line.

The period to which we now turn is that when Egypt was conquered and ruled one hundred years by her mother country, Ethiopia. The two nations were in blood relation to each other just as the Germanic Races of America, England and Germany are related today, and they were in constant war with each other then as these modern nations are now, for the predominance of power and commerce.

History only repeats itself which shows that the man of today regardless of Race, Color or Creed is practically the same man as he was many thousand years ago.

PanKhi, the Nigger King

The 21st Egyptian Dynasty was Ethiopian, it began with the reign of Piankhi. This chapter is titled,

"Nigger King," it is the first time in my life that I have been delighted to use the word "Nigger," and I do it specifically to prove the falsifying of Negro History and to prove to you with reliable data and reference that these Ethiopians and Egyptians were the same people that today we call Negroes. They were not white, they were not yellow, they were black people, the direct ancestors of the African and American Negroes.

In my research in Egyptian antiquity, unexpectingly I came across a volume titled the "Personalities of Antiquity" by Arthur Weigall, Page 185, the 24th chapter, is captioned *The Exploits of a Nigger King*. My first glimpse at this chapter struck me in amazement and curiosity, I wondered why the term "Nigger" was used in a classical text, I was filled with inspiration and delight when I had read it. For the first time in my life, I found the term "Nigger" used to advantage, for it is a rhetorical license to use the strongest term that the subject can bear to bring out its meaning. Mr. Weigall meant no prejudice in the use of the term "Nigger." He knew that if he had used the term Ethiopian, the vast majority of modern writers had already tried to convert the word "Ethiopian" to mean brunette, whites or semite browns, but when he says "Nigger" no one could mistake the meaning. Then if Egypt and Ethiopian had one Negro King they had hundreds.

Mr. Weigall was Inspector General of Antiquity for the Egyptian Government in 1923. He was in the position to give first hand information of reliable data concerning this Ancient African Nation, with such evidence and facts coming from the pen of an outstanding white author, telling the world that PanKhi, the Egyptian Pharoah, was a black man, serves as a great volume of support to the contention of my arguments. It was also of vital interest when I found that a Negro Professor of Ancient History, from a colored university of the United States was the cause of Mr. Weigall's acknowledgment and introduction of PanKhi to the world as a Negro King in no uncertain terms, in Mr. Weigall's own words: "One day in London, a few years ago, I was called upon the telephone by an American unknown to me, he was a professor of Ancient History at a university in the United States. He asked an interview in order to discuss certain archeological matter.

Mr. Weigall continues: "This Professor was well dressed and he was perfectly Black and proved to be a man of a considerable scholarship eager to raise the status of his people."

The mission of this Negro Professor with Mr. Weigall was to find out how that he could "obtain permission to unearth the buried relics of the ancient graves of his dusky forefathers." The noted colored professor whose name the author did not mention and he further says that he did not know whether Negro Historian accomplished his mission or not, but one thing that the Negro Professor did, he impressed the noted English Historian and Archeologist with such eloquent and logical argument with so much interest that it inspired the author to acknowledge that the culture of Ethiopia and Egypt was Negro. The colored Professor also stated in his interview "that it was fitting that a Negro rather

[47]

than a white man should undertake the study of the remains left behind that astonishing Epoch of Negro Dominion."

The Historian Weigall said: "I came to the conclusion that my visitor (Negro Professor) was probably right in his belief that it takes a Negro to understand a Negro."

I felt very fortunate in forwarding the works of Mr. Weigall, being an outstanding Archeologist formerly employed by the Egyptian Government. His testimony on African Archeology and history, gives a substantiated support to the very facts in Negro history for writing this chapter. When an English Archeologist says "that PanKhi was a nigger King." One cannot be mistaken in the meaning—PanKhi, the Priest King, the father of Taharqua and King of Egypt. PanKhi came to the throne of Ethiopia in the year 700 B.C. the capital being the city of Napata, he was a Priest King and devout follower of Amon, who then was God of Ethiopia and Egypt.

The word Amon today is converted to *"Amen— Praise the Lord,"*—in a practical sense, time has little altered its interpretation. Mr. Weigall's acknowledgment that the Ethiopian Kings were Negroes such as King PanKhi and his illustrious Son (Taharqua) gives uncompromising support on the contention of my argument. Mr. Weigall is a noted Englishman, is one of the most outstanding Egyptologists in the world. He spent many years in research and exploration of Egyptian antiquity. He is also a member of the catalogue staff of the museum at Cairo and is the author of eleven books on the antiquity of Egypt. Such an acknowledgment coming from this renown Egyptologist is enough to substantiate my historical stand. It should be remembered that it was a colored Professor, whose name he did not mention, that inspired his acknowledgment of a fact which most modern writers on Egypt and Ethiopia would have us forget.

Mr. Weigall stated that he did not know whether the Professor had been able to fulfill his purpose or not, but if the professor did not accomplish the purpose, there is one thing that he succeeded in his mission of meeting this Egyptologist who had done the excavating of the ancient ruins of the Black Empires of Egypt and Ethiopia and had discovered and was writing to acknowledge the truth that the colored professor was looking for, the grandiloquent and religious annals left by King PanKhi, the most famous of Negro Kings.

Piankhi claimed to be a heavenly born King and predestined by Amon to rule. He organized a powerful army and invaded Egypt with well trained black troops. He ordered his soldiers "when you arrive in Thebes baptize yourselves in Holy water, know that Amon is your God, and that it is he who has sent us—do not boast of your strength for there is no strength but Amon, bow to him saying 'Show us the way that we may fight, in the Shadow of thy Sword.'"

PanKhi may rightfully be called a Hallelujah Pharaoh. He baptized his soldiers before battle and exhorted them to put their trust in Amon to sprinkle themselves with Holy water. Piankhi could conveniently be classed as a Methodist-Baptist King.

He believed in emersion and sprinkling both. After his death he was succeeded by his brother Shabaha.

Shabaha was a great warrior. He engaged the Assyrians in the great battle of Raphia, in which the Assyrian were victorious but not decisive enough for them to invade Egypt. Shabaha appears to have been only a Regent Pharaoh. His reign was temporary until his brother's son Prince Taharqua had reached the age of manhood. Taharqua, it is said, was brought from Ethiopia by his uncle Shabaka at the age of twenty and seized the throne of Egypt.

Nofertumkhira Taharqua ascended the throne of Egypt about 740 B.C. during the most turbulent period of Egyptian history. Taharqua transcended of his father, King PanKhi as a soldier but he was not a Hallelujah man. He was an admirer of Rameses, the Great, and did everything he could to emulate the deeds of the Great Rameses. Taharqua stretched the boundaries of the Egyptian Empire from the Pillars of Hercules to the confines of India. During his reign a great war broke out between Egypt and Assyria. Taharqua led an army of one million black soldiers and engaged the army under the command of Sennacherib at the Battle of Elteka.

In this battle the Ethiopians and Egyptians were under the command of King Taharqua but they were repulsed and Taharqua made a strategical retreat which shortened his line of battle and he fell back to save Egypt from Assyrian invasion. But in the meantime an epidemic broke out among the Assyrian army and the next morning one hundred and eighty-five thousand Assyrian soldiers lay dead upon the ground. Taharqua attributed this disaster to the destruction wrought by the God Amon and the Jews claim that it was Jehovah their God, who sent an angel to slay the enemies of Jerusalem. Sennacherib never attempted another expedition and died soon after. He was succeeded by Assurhaddon, who remembered the disaster that befell the Assyrian army twenty years before; renewed the campaign against Egypt, learning that King Taharqua had organized a vast army to prevent the invasion through the Nile Valley. The Assyrian King changed the route of his expedition and marched directly to the City of Memphis. Taharqua learning the new plan made a counter march to check the attack on Memphis met the Assyrian army with stubborn resistance but the resistance was not strong enough to save Memphis, the city was taken and Taharqua fled to Ethiopia but sickness soon befell King Assurhaddon and he was succeeded by his son Assurbinapol during which time Taharqua redeemed the throne of Egypt and was proclaimed King.

King Assurbanipal renewed the plan to capture Egypt. King Taharqua for the third time drew his sword in the defense of Egypt,—at this time he was advanced in years, but he still had plenty of fight left in him. He engaged the enemies in the Delta of the Nile, this time Taharqua was defeated and he returned to Ethiopia.

The following inscription was found upon the tablets among the ruins of Nineveh some years ago, King Assurbanipals, description of Taharqua: "Taharqua, King of Muser (Egypt) and (Kusi) Ethiopia, defied the Gods of our fathers. He put motion in his own strength to take possession of Egypt. He disregarded the commandments of the Great God Assur. He trusted in his strength and did not observe the treaty he made with my father who begat me had made with him.

Mr. Arthur Weigall's book *The Personalities of Antiquity* (Page 192) says: "Taharqua, who is mentioned in the Bible, 2 Kings 19:9, and whose portrait-statue shows him to have been a full blooded Negro, was uncommonly like the American (Negro Professor) who came to call on me."

I have seen the Picture of Taharqua myself wearing a Leopard's coat, complexion jet black with definite Negro features, that would very strongly compare with the Prophet Jeremiah's remarks "Can an Ethiopian change his skin or a Leopard his spots." Taharqua invasion of Asia is spoken of in 2 Kings of the Bible.

5

Black Egypt
and Her Negro Pharaohs

My interest in writing this chapter with the finding of many things, which I believed to be true, but I did not have enough evidence to support my claim.

In my research I became very much interested when I succeeded in finding and collecting enough data from some of the most outstanding historians, and anthropologists both ancient and modern, and also the history recorded on monuments—reliable evidence of facts on ancient Egyptian civilization and the race to which they belong.

Millions of dollars have been spent in expeditions and explorations to find and unearth the marvelous wonders of the Land of the Pharaoh's, but with a few exceptions, these scientists have failed to tell the Racial background or the merits of the ancient Egyptian culture and the characteristics of its people.

Many of these writers, both in school text books and general history, refer to the ancient Egyptians as a white race; more or less as semitic stock, using the term which has become a slogan in all such histories, "that the ancient Egyptians were not Negroes."

In my reply to these authors' false statements, I will say frankly that the ancient Egyptians were not a Caucasian, nor a Semitic Race, but they were full blooded Negroes, and belonged to the same race of Negroes that you find in America and Africa today.

The ancient Egyptians were black with woolly hair and thick lips, similar to what you would find in the colored race today; while I admit that in some of them in the northern section of Egypt, the shades of complexion were somewhat brown in color, while on the other hand those who lived in the southern parts of Egypt were darker because of the vertical rays of the sun.

The varied complexions of the African Nations up to the period of 700 B.C. was caused by the variation of climate, and the high altitude of mountain chains rather than the admixture of Race.

The ancient Egyptians were not white nor yellow, and in this chapter I take great pride to introduce them to the world as a nation of Black men; there were no mixed breeds found among them until the later period of the Empire.

The ancient Egyptian Empire was founded and built by Black men who ruled and governed Egypt for several thousands years without foreign interference, with exception of the time she was invaded by HyKsos and Ethiopia, but the two black nations were members of the same race.

The Egyptians descended from the Ethiopians: Heeren's *Historical Research of African Nation,*

Pages 313-14, says: "Thebes, as well as the states in general of upper Egypt, are called in the proper annals of the Priest colonies from Meroe in Ethiopia; and at Thebes the service of Jupiter-Amon, whose temple was the common center of the State, gives itself a striking evidence of such was the case—Memphis, whose situation was so remarkable from dam and embankments is called a colony of Thebes. The other cities of Egypt likewise derive their descent—directly or indirectly—from Ethiopia of which they considered themselves as colonies and of which their religion and institution furnished abundant proofs."

From the body evidence then we come to the conclusion that the same race which ruled in Ethiopia and Meroe, spread themselves as colonies, in the first instance in upper Egypt, that these later colonies in consequence of their great prosperity in their turn was the parent body of the other."

The Scientist Pritchard in his *Natural History of Man*, Page 153, says: "The true Negro confirmation requires no comment, but the practical eye readily detects a few heads with decidedly mixed character in which those of the Negro predominates. For these I propose the name of the Negroid Crania. For while ostealogical development is more or less that of the Negro, the hair is long but sometimes harsh, thus indicating the combination of features which is familiar in the mulatto of the present day. There remains other examples in which the Caucasian traits predominate but it is partially blended with those of the Negro."

The Historian Pritchard in the above paragraph

[55]

tried his best to make a Caucasian out of the ancient Egyptian. The more he tried to make him white, the blacker he turned.

Pritchard begins his argument with the Egyptian being a Negro and ends where he begins—the Egyptian being a Negro.

While I will admit that these found in Egypt, the mummies, of kings that were not black Egyptians or what we call Negroes, but these mummies, if found, were the kings who ruled Egypt after the fall of Ethiopia and Egyptian Pharaohs—because Egypt and Ethiopia were great Empires of the Black Nation.

Pritchard further says, Pages 124-5: "In their complexion and in many of their physical peculiarities, the Egyptians were an African Race, in the Eastern and even in the Central parts of Africa, we shall trace the existence of various groups in physical character, nearly resembling the Egyptians, and it would be difficult to observe a gradual deviation among many African nations of that continent from the physical type of the Egyptians, to the strongly marked character of the Negro, without any very decided break or interruption."

In the above paragraph Pritchard shows plainly that these Egyptians were a Negro Race and the gradual change in the complexion of the African nation is due directly from climatic influence but they belong to the same stock.

Rallingsons in his *History of Egypt,* Page 24, says: "It is even conceivable that the Egyptians was produced by a gradual advance and Amelioration from that of the Negro."

[56]

The Scientist Massey in his book *Egypt the Light of the World,* Page 251, says: "The dignity is so ancient that the insignia of the Pharaohs evidently belong to a time when the Egyptians wore nothing but the girdle of the Negro."

Captain Burton, an English explorer, in 1883 wrote Massey, saying: "You are quite right about the African origin of the Egyptian. I have sent home a hundred skulls to prove it."

The Greek Herodatus says: "The Colchian certainly appear to be of Egyptian origin which indeed before I had conversed with any on the subject I had always believed. But I was desirous of being satisfied. I interrogated the people of both countries and the results were, it seemed that Colchian had better remembrance of the Egyptian than the Egyptian had of the Colchian. The Egyptians were of the opinion that the Colchians were descended from the troops of Sesostris' army. To this I was also inclined because they were black and their hair was short and curled."

The Scientist Volney says: "The ancient Egyptians were real Negroes of the same species with all the natives of Africa and though as it might be expected, after mixture for many ages with the Greeks and Romans, they have lost their identity of their first color, yet they still retain strong marks of their first conformation."

Brusch, *Egypt Under the Pharaohs,* page 401, says: "I have expressed the opinion that the Egyptian migrated from a primeval home in Asia, yet this idea is opposed by another view—by a method of historical data that the origin of the Egyptian

[57]

people would have to be sought in the Nigritian (Negro) Baraba (Africa). These are supposed to have ascended the upper Nile Valley from the South and to have cultivated it and created one of the few centuries of civilization in the ancient world, without losing or renouncing the peculiarities of their African Custom. Their mingling with a Syro-Abrabian nomad Race who penetrated Egypt from the East and also with the Libyan from the West is supposed to have given origin to the Egyptian of today in which the African Blood predominates."

The Black Pharaohs of the 18th Dynasty

The 18th Dynasty is said to have been the Golden Age of Egyptian history. This dynasty was founded by an Ethiopian Princess, Nefertari; through her marriage to the Egyptian King Aahmes the 1st, Rallinson says: "The complexion of the Ethiopian queen was ebon blackness"; and that she had the most attractive personality and was called the beautiful companion of Aahmes."

She was the most venerated woman in Egyptian history. She was called the wife of the God Amon and the Ancestress of the 18th Dynasty which marked the glorious period in Egyptian annals.

Budge's *History of Egypt* in Vol. A, page 182-3, says: "It has often been said that the period of the 12th Dynasty was the Golden Age of Egypt, but if a nation's greatness is to be rated by its material, wealth and power, this title will be more justly applied to the period of the 18th Dynasty which undoubtedly marks the highest point which Egypt's civilization and power had ever reached."

[58]

During the joint reign of Queen Neferti and King Aahmes, Ethiopia and Egypt became allied powers and these two Black Nations together drove out the Shepherd Kings from Egypt which had ruled the Nile Delta for a long period of time. The aid of this black queen restored Egypt to her former glory.

The reason the names of the Pharaohs of the 18th assumed the name of Amonotep or Amenophis, their Ancestrial National line from their Mother. Queen Neferti bore the title as the wife of the God Amon and her son and three other princes of this dynasty assume the name of Amenotep or Amenotepti, meaning the "Sons of Amon." Aahmes—Neferti's reign was succeeded by their son, who ascended the throne as Amenophis the first. He was a great promoter of art and peace and his name occurs on General monuments in Egypt.

Amenophis also married a Princess from Ethiopia whose name was Neferti, similar to the name of his mother, the name Neferti was commonly known to the Egyptian queens.

Amenophis 1st, was succeeded by his son Thotmes 1st, who was a Negro Pharoah. Rallinson says that the Black blood "showed itself in the countenance where the short depressed flat nose and unduly thick lips are of the Cushite (Ethiopia) rather than Egyptian type."

Rallingson, *Story of Ancient Egypt,* page 158: "I admit there was some difference in the expression of the Egyptian and Ethiopian, just as one may be able to detect the difference between the nations of northern and southern Europe, but the

[59]

differences lie in the degree of climate rather than race. The Ethiopians being nearer the Equator, were darker than the Egyptian. The word 'Egypt' means black, Ethiopia means sun burnt—but both the Egyptian and Ethiopian were Negroes.

Thotmes 1st was succeeded by his son Thotmes 2nd whose reign was very short, and he seemed to have reigned jointly with his sister, and his power and influence were circumscribed and over-shadowed by his sister-queen.

"Thotmes 2nd was succeeded by his son Thotmes 3rd who was called the 'Alexander the Great of Egypt.' This Pharoah conquered the known world and caused the names of six hundred and twenty-eight different nations to be carved upon the walls of Karnak and a tablet of Victory to be set in the Temple.

Thothmes 3rd fought the Battle of the World's First Armageddon, which derived its name from a very ancient city in Palestine, Megiddo, just beyond the River Jordon, and the Sea of Galilee, fifteen miles south of the town Nazareth, where Jesus Christ, the Son of God, spent his childhood years."

This first battle of Armageddon was fought nearly fifteen hundred years before Christ. It was so decisive and disastrous that Bible students claims that it inspired the Prophet Ezekiel in the vision of dry bones and also St. John, the seer of Patmos Isle, as prototype of the world's future and last most terrible Battle which is most likely to get its fulfillment in the present World War. It should be remembered that the world's first Armageddon was fought by the Black Thothmes, and even in this present world conflict the Armageddon that is now being fought, and Ethiopian. Halie Selassie, was its first challenge.

Thothmes, 3rd, was succeeded by his son, Amenophis, 2nd; Amenophis, 2nd, was succeeded by his son Thothmes the 4th, who married an Ethiopian woman, she may have been a Princess, but as to her social status, history is silent, but it does say that she was an Ethiopian, mother of Amenophis, 3rd, the son of Thothmes, 4th—Wikerson in his book *Ancient Egypt,* page 42, says of the features of Amenophis, 3rd:

"The features of this monarch cannot fail to strike everyone who examines the portraits of the Egyptian Kings, as having more in common with the Negro than of any other Pharaoh—in consequence of his mother being Ethiopian origin."

Rollingson says in his book *Ancient Egypt,* Vol. 2, page 271, "Amenophis, the 3rd, was succeeded by his son Thothmes the 4th, he was also a Black Pharoah. His mother seems to have been from the Galla tribes of Ethiopia; he is supposed to have derived his strange physique from his maternal ancestors who are thought to have been an Abyssinian of the Galla family.

Thothmes, 4th, was succeeded by his son Amenophis, 4th; Amenophis, 4th, it is said by some historian, was influenced by Jewish ideas of religion and assumed the name Khuenaten—"the believer of one God," which rendered him very unpopular with his people.

His reign was very unpopular, he had three

daughters and died leaving no male heir to his throne. It was a custom that when a Pharaoh died leaving no male heir, the son-in-law became a Pharoah through marriage. The daughter of Khuenaten, married an Ethiopian nobleman, who was the viceroy of a southern province in Egypt, his name was Hi or Hiu who became known later as Tut-Ank-Amon.

Tut-Ank-Amon was a full blooded Negro, and Ethiopian by birth and blood.

Brugsch-Bey in Volume *Egypt Under the Pharoahs,* pages 5-10-12, says it without telling it. "Tut-Ank-Amen" is called the Royal son of Kush," meaning Ethiopia.

Henry Brugsch-Bey further states, "That is the arrival of the splendid Ethiopian tribut, the best selection of the product of the lands of the south, and their landing in Thebes under the conduct of the Royal Son of Kush." The Historian Henry Brugsch-Bey continues: "Even at this day, the prejudice that the Negro both in taste and art, was an unprogressive son of Adam, can be refuted by a hundred facts which prove the direct contrary in an unconvertible manner, in favor of our colored brethren, Tut-Ank-Amon whose very name serves a proof that he had thrown aside the new teachings of his Royal father-in-law about the one living son Disk, reign in Thebes with the consent and the co-operation of the Priest of Amon, by a brilliant external promp. He seems to have obtained the power and respect which were denied him on the account of birth and marriage."

"Tut-Ank-Amon was a great politician and as

well a statesman, when ascending the throne of Egypt, found the country much out of harmony because of the reign of his father-in-law Khuetean, the former Amenophis 4th, because his heresy in religion."

In order to restore national unity in Egypt, he went back to the original faith of Egypt and Ethiopia and restored the worship of Amon while he assumed the name Tut-Ank-Amon, which means the living image of Amon. He restored Thebes to her former glory, with perfect unity throughout the Empire.

In his brief but glorious reign, Egypt was at peace with all nations and Thebes was a world's capital, which is better described in the line of Homer:

Not all proud Thebes unrivaled walls contain
The World's great Empress of the Egyptian plain,
That spreads her conquest over a thousand states
And pours her heroes through a hundred gates.

Lord Carnarvon the archangel of the scientific world, has done a great thing. When he found the tomb of this Ethiopian Pharaoh, Tut-Ank-Amon, it showed the American Negro the solution of his problem in the resurrection of a Black King.

Africa is ours today as she was yesterday when Tut-Ank-Amon reigned in Thebes; we can not pay him homages as our Ethiopian ancestors did thousands of years ago, but we can help to redeem Africa and reclaim the continent and bring

[63]

back the prestige of a lost civilization that gave to the world the first light of intelligence. Africa is ours and the spirit of Tut-Ank-Amon yet lives.

The Negro Pharaoh of the 19th Dynasty

Heeren, in *Research of African Nations*, page 426, tells that Amenopnis 3rd was the father of Rameses, the great, and that Amepohis 3rd had more in common with Negro features than any other Pharaoh.

Heeren's chronological tables close the 18th Dynasty with the reign of Amenophis 3rd, while other historians close it with the reign of Tut-Ank-Amen; but Rallinson agrees with Heeren that Amenophis 3rd was of Negro blood, it is not ours to argue the founder of contested chronologies of the various dynasties; be that as it may.

My only purpose and aim is to show, and to prove that these Egyptian Pharaohs were Negro kings. It is said that during the reign of Amenophis, 3rd of the 18th Dynasty, that the Hyksos or Shepherd Kings of Asia, threatened Egypt with a record invasion. Heeren says "Amenophis, 3rd, not thinking himself able to withstand them confided his son Rameses, five years of age, to a friend in Ethiopia—to a King which was a tributary and friendly towards him. He assembled his forces and marched back to Egypt, assisted by his son and successor, expelled the conquering Shepherds."

At the head of the 19th Dynasty stands the name of the most celebrated of all Pharaohs. He is called Sesostris, or Sesostrus or Rameses, the Great.

Manetho informs us and other writers alive

attest that the son of Amenophis was called Rameses—the father of Rameses the Great was a Negro King. Rameses the Great was the father of the Great Seti; and Seti was the father of Rameses 2nd. The Great Seti was a black king.

Rallinson in his *Story of Ancient Egypt,* page 252, says that "Seti's face was thoroughly African. Strong, fierce, with depressed flat nose, thick lips and heavy chin." We may conclude that Seti was of the thoroughly African Race with perhaps, an admixture of more southern blood; which means Ethiopia. "Seti was the father of Rameses 2nd."

6

The Black Race as Parent Stock

For many thousand years the Black race was the only people to inhabit the whole earth and even today the Negro Race stretches around the whole earth at the equator regardles of the different color and varieties of other nations. The world still wears a Black Belt. The far-flung Black belt of the world had its beginning in the native confines of Africa which includes ninety per cent of the African continent and stretches itself clear across the continent of Southern Asia to Australia, the Islands of the Pacific and to the shores of Central and South America.

The Negro race today is one of the largest divisions of the human family on earth. The black population of Africa is under-estimated by modern geographers who claim that there are only one hundred fifty million people in Africa of the black race. This statement is a joke for according to the Paris Geographical Society, 1900, it was estimated that the black population of Africa was four hundred million; this number is in addition to the vast stretch of the Black Belt through Asia, India, Australia, the Pacific and America.   There are at least eight hundred million of Negro or Negroids in the world, approaching nearly one half of the two billion people who live on the planet today.   While on the other hand the Brown, the Yellow and White Races are branches from this Black Parent Stock.   The races of man separated at some remote period and the change in color and features was caused by climatic environments.

Ancient Landmarks and Traditional Mountains

Ancient landmarks are the lines which we shall now follow, the trail of the most ancient Pilgrimage of the nations of the earth.   Nature and tradition have left an index of the migration of prehistoric man, if we would but notice the different land marks where the nations formed themselves into separate groups, after leaving Ethiopia (Africa) the mother country of the world.

I have already shown and proven that the black race was the first and oldest stock of the human family.   Our next argument is to show and prove that this race is the parent stock of all others.   We will build our hypothesis from three main basic facts, (A) Negro Aborigines or native races are found all around the globe, their population followed the equator, encircled the earth and the sun never sets on a Negro or Negroid child.   (B) The most ancient monuments, and Fossils and Statues of Ancient gods that are found on every continent are Negroes, and monuments tell a truth that critics cannot defy; monuments are living witnesses of an established fact and portray the features as likenesses of the people who erected them. (C) The Ancient Skeleton of Prehistoric man wherever found is Negroid. Dr. Gerald Massey in his book *"Egypt the Light of the World"*—Page 250 says: "The one sole race that can be traced all over the earth above or below the ground is the dark race of the dwarf Negrito type and the only one possible mother land for these preliminary people is Africa."

Black Race in Asia

(1) At a very remote period the blacks migrated from Africa founded Great Empires and built great cities in Asia. The Great Babylonian Empire was founded by them. The Chaldeans gave themselves out as a colony of the Egyptian and there can be no doubt that their culture stood closely with that of Egypt. *History of Mankind,* by Ratzell—page 547. Of the first Chaldean Empire, of which Babylon was the Capital, Mespero says: That "a Negritic people inhabited a considerable portion of Asia in Prehistoric times."

All the near East was peopled by the Black Race such as the Empires of Babylon, Assyria and Tyre and other lesser States were ruled by them.

The Jewish Nation

The Jews were the first nation to branch off from the Black and the most striking proofs of this fact is that there are Black Jews still found in Africa and India. They have their Asiatic features and speak the Hebrew language, and I have often heard they are more accurate in their tradition than many Jews elsewhere. The African and Indian

Jews belong to the branch that left the UR of the Chaldees with Abraham. I had an occasion to meet a Black Rabbi from Ethiopia and talked with him at length, and he told me that the Jews and the African people are but one race and the Jews were originally black but grew lighter living in Gentile countries where the climate was much colder than in Africa.

A. H. Keen in his book titled *Stanford Compendium of Geography and African Travels* says: "Indeed the opinion is daily gaining ground amongst Philogists that the Semites and Hamites were originally but one people."

Moses in the book of *Genesis* 11:31, 12:1 corroborates Dr. Keen's statement when he says, "And Terah took Abraham his son and Lot the son of Haran his son's son and Sara his daughter-in-law, Abraham's wife and they went forth with them from the Ur of the Chaldees to go into the land of Canaan and into Huran and dwelt there. Now the Lord said unto Abraham get thee out of thy country from thy kindred and from thy father's house unto the land that I will show thee.

The Chaldeans were a Kushite nation and the word Kush is a Hebrew word for Ethiopia which shows that the Jews descended from the Ethiopian Race.

Marcus Dourd in his volume *Bible Expositor* says: This people (Jews) say their old writings are descended from the Chaldeans; they sojourned heretofore in Mesopotamia because they will not follow the gods of their fathers.

The Hindo Kush Mountain
The Black Race in India

The Black Race inhabited all the land in the near East in Asia but in their migration into Central, Southern and far Eastern portions of the continent, the climate changed them into new racial types. India which begins at the southern side of the Hindo-Kush mountains (a range of mountains five hundred miles in length) which is traditionally the place of the beginning of the Hindo People of India, the place where the Ethiopia Race formed itself into the Hindu or Indian nation. Victor Dury, a French author in his volume *Ancient History of the East*—Vol. 1, Page 21 says, "India was first peopled by a Black Race—with whom Herodotus was acquainted in Cedrosia under the name Ethiopians." According to the *Cambridge Ancient History*, Volume 1, page 21: "The Geographical severance at the narrow and almost impassable neck of high land, where the Hindu Kush intervenes between Afghanistan and Pamirs has its human counter part in the segregation of the Ancestors of the yellow skinned, straight-haired Mongoloid stock from all westerly varieties. In the same way the correlation of the black-skinned, wooly haired stocks with the Malayan fauna which is suggested by their actual distribution, would seem to postulate a period of time comparable with that suggested above for the Mongoloid within which no less, highly specialized Negroid physique could be developed from a precursor more widely distributed, especially north-westward presenting those features in which both Negroid and White stocks differ from the Yellow." It is most likely at this point marked the Traditional Land, marked where the climate was somewhat modified that the Cushite (Ethiopian) became Hindu in nationality but there was either little difference in the climate of India and Africa that change is just enough to show that the subcontinent is a branch of the Ethiopian Race. The continent is over one-third Negroid today." Dr. Badha Kunrud Mookadi, Professor of Indian History at the University of Lucknor in his book *Hindo Civilization,* page 33, says: "The earlist people to occupy India are supposed to belong to the Nigritic Race."

Prof. Ernest A. Hooten the anthropologist of Harvard University, page 543, says: "When you reach India and go from the north to the south in that vast peninsula the Negroid strain in the population everywhere perceptible becomes more and more marked." Out of the four hundred million people of India at least thirty per cent of the vast population could easily be classed as Negroids. Ancient India once was called Ethiopia. The Greek Historian Herodotus, the most reliable historian of all the world on Egypt and Ethiopia, for he was an eye witness on the scene, says: "That the Ethiopian Race inhabited the lands toward the rising and setting sun. He divided them into two nations and said they differed in nothing from the other Ethiopian save their language and the character of their hair." Also we might mention the Statue of Buddha with Negroid features is found throughout India which shows that wooly haired race once

[71]

ruled there. This Greek Historian says, the Eastern Ethiopians have straight hair while they of Libya (Africa) are more wooly than any other nation on earth.

It is also with much interest when we quote the words of Herodotus because as Professor Latham in his volume, *Man and His Migration,* says: "The nine books of Herodotus form the most ethonological work not written by a professer and conscious ethonologist. Herodotus was an unconscious, an instinctive one and his ethnology was sufficiently comprehensive in character—let his name always be mentioned with his work." His works were written as an eye witness to the scene and he had no such thing as we find today, his work was void of racial bias.

So as to India he speaks of the Ethiopian population south of the Hindu-Kush mountain as being the Eastern Ethiopian, black with straight hair but was of the same ethnogical strain as the black Ethiopian in Africa. The Ancient Empire of Ethiopia once included all the subcontinent of India. Professor Latham says of the population, "the foreign element is manifested less than in the north. So it is the south of India which exhibits the original in its fullest form. In respect the Southern Indian is darker than the Northern." But he refers to the population along the northern part of India as being Persian extraction which somewhat lighter in complexion—but depart from it in comparison against themselves. If the lips are thick and skin black we think of the Negro.

Black Men in Persia

There are clear signs of Negro mixture in Persia and in India there are traces of intermingling with the Negro race to which fact the darkness of the skin color so widely prevalent may be attributed—*Human History* by Eliot Smith, page 126.

Negroid in Arabia

As to Arabia the Negro extraction needs no comment for from time immemorial the Arabs have been a sub-Egyptian people constantly mixing with the black of Africa until today in Southern Arabia as well in other portions of the country the Arab is very Negroid.

Negroids in Indo-China

Indo-China is a landmark in the beginning of the Chinese Nation, I find that Indo-China like India was first inhabited by a Negritic type of people, the same as you will find today throughout the South Pacific Islands. The Negritos probably come to China by the way of India. The anthropologists say, there is some reason to believe that southern China in times more recent than the old Stone Age in Europe was occupied by a race of Negroid curly haired pygmies like those still existing in the out way Philippines, New Guinea and elsewhere.

According to Ancient Relics found in China and the present Negroid strains found along the Chinese Tibetan border that Chinese Border Race evolved from the Ethiopian—Negroid Stock. Later on, in another period you notice in Chinese culture, that there was another wave of black migration that came to China from the Land of Chaldee they were more cultured than China's primitive inhabitants, and conquered them, and gave them speech and culture. These blacks were the founders of the Ancient Chinese Empire whose history is almost as remote as that of Egypt and Babylon. Some historians have tried to prove that China has a greater antiquity than Egypt or Babylon, but they have not been able to gather enough material to establish their contention. I prefer to stand with reliable data rather than jump to absurd conclusions. I feel safe in saying that ancient Chinese Empire, according to Dr. Charles Gutzlaff, in *History of China* was founded in the 2205 B.C. and he farther says any date of this nation that goes back farther than above record is "extravagant and unfounded." The Chinese seem to have derived the blue print of their culture from Chaldea who was a Kushite or Ethiopian Nation, the founders of the Babylonian Empire. The Babylonians erected walls around their cities, but the Chinese instead built great massive walls around their entire country, the Chinese learn this wall building from their ancient forefathers of the near East. The Chinese were wise in one point of view but weak in another. They realized that in time of war with a wall built around a city only, the enemy could stage a long siege against it and starve out the population, but on the other hand the massive walls protected China but shut her in from the world so that her civilization grew stagnant and died. Another reason for saying that the Chinese culture came from Chaldee is because of such names as China, Chung, Chung-king and Chang which is similar to Chaldee.

Professor Willis Broughton in *History of Ancient People,* page 58, says: "The inhabitants of China are of the yellow race type but no doubt build upon a black foundation. The ethnologist found there the evidence of remote Pigmy or Negroid population."

Pritchard in his *Natural History of Man,* page 237 says: "The Aborigines of Cochin-China are called Mays and are the people which inhabit the chain of mountain which separate it from Cambodia —They are a race of people very black and resemble the features of the Kaffir (South Africa) the Cochin-Chinese. They resemble them in their features and their custom."

Negroes in Indo-Malaya

The Negroid tribes migrating to Southwestern Asia where the climate had undergone very little if any change to its ancient motherland, Africa, evolved into what is known as the Malayan. These tribes arrived at two respective points, the first I have already described as Indo-China where it merged itself into the Chinese group, another wave of black proceeded to move in a southeastern direction reaching the point of division known as Indo-Malaya. In the volume *Man From the Farthest Past,* page 301, it is stated: "It now seems probable that the whole of Southern Asia then contained a sparse population of people belonging to the black skinned races, which we find today in various forms in Africa, India and some of the Islands stretching out in the South East of Asia."

These Negroid tribes arriving at this point split

[75]

into parts, known as the Negroid and the Malay, but I only use the term Malay from an accommodative sense, authentically speaking there is no such race as Malay; the so called Malay is an off-shoot branch of the black. The Malay betrays that name by having African features.

Negroids in Australia

The Negroes are found throughout the East Indies Islands some of them are lighter than others with hair less wooly and sometimes curly. This line of Oceanic Negroes stretches across the Pacific to the continent of South America, they are found in the Philippines, and the Japanese Island of Formosa.

Eliot Smith in his book *Human History*, page 125, says: "The other great mass of the Negro race occupies New Guinea spreads through the Melenesian, the Bismark Archipelago, New Caledonia, the Fiji, even to the Islands far out in Eastern Polynesia and the American coast."

Ellen Semple in her volume *The Influence of Geographical Environment*, page 161, says: "The Negroids are dispersed in eight provinces of Luzon and in several other Islands." The volume also says, "Negroids are in the Japanese Island of Formosa, but the Negritos crop out again in the mountain and interior of Formosa and in Borneo".

And T. T. Waterman, in his book *The Source of Anthropology*, page 161, call them the "Afro-Malaysian type and includes as well the Malaysian people, the Malay, Javanese and Sumatrian".

Negroids in.the Philippines and Japan

While the Japanese have been classified as belonging to the yellow race recent research has found the Japanese to be an offshoot of the Malayan race. Colonel A. Brighane in *Shadow of the Atlantis,* page 188, says: "The nose of the Basques are sometime eagle type like Mayan nose but the Japanese nose is flat. Moreover the language has some anologies with Malayan and Polynesian tongue circumstated with some physical peculiarities of the Japanese, this has induced many anthropologist to ascribe this nation to the Malayan race.

H. C. Wells in *Outline of History,* page 1160, in his discription of the Japanese says: "It is not impossible that they are a back-flow from the Trans-Pacific drift of the early heliclithic culture, but they may also have absorbed from the south Malay and Negrito elements; Negro blood is also found in the Hawaiian Island."

The Negro and Negroid population extend around the world and belt the globe.

We conclude this chapter with an analogy quoted from *Cambridge Ancient History* that the blood of the Prehistoric black race is found on every continent and island today.

Cambridge Ancient History, pages 27 and 28, says: "Analogous local adaptation of a generically African type associated in its geographical range with survivor of an African Faunna may be regarded as sufficiently accounting for the oceanic Negroes for the Negroid Dravidian survival in southern India and beyond for the ancient description of the

[77]

Asiatic Ethiopians. In Mekran· and in extreme South Arabia around the margin of sunken regions of Indo-Africa and for the curious survival in the Mediterranean and even in France and Britain of type which combine certain characteristics of Negro and white man without any of the common marks of the half breed."

Negroids—Sir Harry Johnson in his *Negro in the New World,* page 25, 26, 27, says:

The Negroids types would seem (judging from the skulls and skeleton remains) have penetrated north westwards as far as Brittany and quite possible as far as Britain and Ireland. Eastward it is traceable through Switzerland and Italy, coming through the Neolithic Period and fusing with northern races.

In modern times and at the present day, it is obvious there is an old Nigretic element in the population of North Africa, Spain, France, Ireland and West Britain, Italy, Sardonic and Sicily and the countries bordering the eastern Mediterranean. Not entirely to be accounted for by the historical slave trade—Negroids elements permeate the tribes of western and eastern India, penetrate the coast tribes of southern Persia to eastern Arabia, invading Burma and the Malay Peninsula, the Philippine Islands, traces its passage through Sumatra, Borneo and the Island of Timor and so in New Guinea, the existing population of Solomon Islands, New Ireland and Hebrides and perhaps the people of New Ireland are the most nearly akin to the African Negro of all Asiatic or Australian people.

Asiatic Negroes also seem to have entered Australia from New Guinea.

A Negroid element in (Melenisian) Fiji as far west as Hawaii Archepelago in Burma Formosa Rin-Kin Island and Southern Japan.

The elements of Mesopatamia appear to have been a Negroid people with kinky hair and to have transmitted their racial type to the Jews and Syrians.

There is a curliness of hair together with a Negro eye and full lips in the portraiture of Assyria which conveys the idea of an evident Negro element in Babylonia.

7

Negroes in Ancient Europe

The Caucausin Mountain—the Ancient Land Mark.

The Caucaus Mountain is the ancient land mark which is the Continental Divide separating Europe from Asia and it also marks the beginning of a race that is known as the Caucasian or White Race. While the Caucaus Mountains stands as Continental Divide it by no means serves as the only entrance or a gate-way to Europe.

When the continent was first peopled or colonized the early inhabitants of Europe were neither yellow nor white, they were a Negroid people who came up out of Africa.

F. Frieman in his volume *Yaradie—A Plea for Africa*, page 54, says: "The fact well attested by history that Ethiopia once bore sway not only in all Africa but almost in all Asia and it is said even two continents could not afford enough for the expansion of their energies. They found their way into Europe and made settlements in Spain and it was then called 'Iherian Ethiopia'."

Frederick Ratzel in his book *The History of Mankind,* quotes Jezul Jones book *Oratrio Dominica,* says: "That he found the Race of Iberian at the foot of the Caucaus Mountains who came from Iberia and Spain and was of African origin". While there is an established school of thought that the Caucausian Race had its beginning in Asia, and they have been classified as Indo-European, but the historian and anthropologists who make such claims have not enough evidence to support their arguments. For most of the prehistoric fossils, implements and skeletons of ancient man that have been found in Europe from the remote periods up until now have been unmistakably proven to be Negroid. Beyond the times of the notorious Ghenchis Khan, the Mongol War Lord and the invasion of Attila, the mad King of the Huns. We have no evidence in history nor anthropology of any prehistoric invasion from Asia. Professor Albert Hooten, Professor of Anthropology at Harvard University in his book *Up from the Ape,* page 577, says: "There is no skeleton evidence of early arrival of the yellow races in Europe." But there have been found plenty skeletons of the black races in Europe.

The primitive or prehistoric man in Europe have been specified in several types as follows: The Piltdown man, Neanderthal, the Cro-Magnon, and the Grimaldi which have supposed to have lived in Europe at more or less different periods in different portions of the continents, but they have been proven to be Negroids skeletons.

A. C. Hadden in his volume *Wandering of Peoples,* pages 39 and 40, says: "Although the arch-

aeologist of Europe has been better studied than that
of any portion of the Old World we cannot recover
the complete history of the people. It is impossible
to deal profitably with the periods preceding the
Paleolithic Age—the earliest phase of which was
marked by crude stone of which the counterparts
are widely spread in Africa and are numerous as
far as India. The remains of a race exhibiting
Negroid features has been found in a cave at Crim-
alda near Mentone, Italy."

Mr. Hadden says although the Archeology of
Europe has been better studied than any portion
of the old world, "but we cannot recover the complete history of its people" but Mr. Hadden does
recover its history, when he tells a fact without admitting it when he speaks of the rude stone implements found in Europe and their counterparts
in Africa and Asia and the Negroid skulls found
near Mentone, Italy.

Professor Willis Broughton in his book *The His
tory of Ancient People,* pages 334-37, says: "Archaeologist have found remains of three races in Europe.
Two of these are generally classed as blacks, may
be known as the Constandt and the Cro-Magnon
Race. But with the Cro-Magnon man black supremacy in Europe came to an end. The climate
change, the black dispersed became the basal elements in the dark branches of the yellow and white
races."

Broughton says: "The climate change the black
dispersed, but the blacks did not disperse, but according to the thermometer the weather black complexion change, without that they could not have

[82]

became the basal elements of the dark yellow and the dark branches of the white race."

Professor Broughton in *History of Ancient People*, page 524, says: "It is believed however that environment has had a changing influence upon all animals, why not on man? The stratum of the blacks would not be subject to the same environment in all regions, differences in blacks would easy arise. They were nomads wandering people."

Sir Arthur Keith in his book, page 385, *New Discoveries Relating to the Antiquity of Man*, writing of the prehistoric Negroids skeleton, says: "I am glad to find that Professor Eliot and Dr. Marat agree with me in this—that there is no good reason for separating the so-called Negroid from other members of the Cro-Magnon stock they have essentially the same features of that stock." The finding of Sir Arthur Keith shows that the Cro-Magnon race in Europe was Negroid also.

Paul Radin in his book *Racial Myth* says that the white race descended from the Cro-Magnon race which inhabited Europe, twenty-five thousand years ago. Sir Arthur Keith also says in his book *New Discoveries Relating to the Antiquity of Man*, page 385, "that we must explain the origin on evolutionary bases, we presume that black, yellow and white are traceable back to a common ancestor in which was combined actually or potentially the character which ultimately becomes differentiated in black, yellow and white races. We should find in the forerunner of the white race some negroids traits of a common ancestor, there is a strong school of thought which regards Africa

[83]

as the most likely homeland of the Caucausin stock both ancient and modern."

Ellen Churchill Semple in the book titled *The Influence of Geographic Environments,* page 121, says: "The long headed (Germanic Race) of northern Europe is regarded now by ethnologist as a short of the long headed brunette Mediterranean Race of African origin which bleached out under the pale sun of the Scandinavian skies."

A dalichociphalic sub-statum of the population with a Negroid type of skull have in fact been found all over Europe through early and the late stone age. Since there is no evidence of any skeleton or implements have been found in Europe during the old and the new stone age, which makes it a geological and historical fact that the black races of Africa were the true ancestors of the races of Europe. The original name of Spain was known as Iberian Ethiopia and Spain and Portugal are known to this day as the "Iberian Peninsular". It would be logical for a historian to believe that the Iberian Ethiopian was an ancient Africian race that came across from Western Africa most likely from the Province of Nigeria. There is a tribe in Africa that is known as Ibos. G. T. Basden in his book *Ibos of Nigeria,* page 31, says: "The color that their complexion variation from light olive to deepest black." But further research shows that the Iberian of Europe descended from the old Cromagnon black stock that flourished in Europe twenty-five thousand years ago.

When Julius Caesar found a vast population of dark complexion known as Gauls, which at that time the Iberian inhabited over Southern half of France and spreading themselves beyond the Pyrenees Mountain including all the Peninsular of Spain and Portugal. The Roman historian Tacitus describes these Iberians as a black skin, curly headed people. There is also a tribe in Ethiopia today known as Gallas which bear almost the same name as Gaul. There is a river in France called the Somme. There is a section of country in East Africa known as Somaliland. Gaul and Galla, Somme and Somaliland correlated terms.

I have not been able to find any evidence in ancient nor Geological History concerning any Indian invasion of Europe during prehistoric times, but have found volumes of reliable records that Europe's early settlers came up out of Africa.

I am positive in saying that there could not have been any Indo-Invasion in Europe during this paleolithic period because the race of man had not then differentiated. Cambridge Ancient History says: "The connecting links between the paleolithic series of the Nile Valley and of western Europe are not yet numerous but enough has been found especially in Algeria—South Tunisia to support the conclusion drawn from the climatic regime—that a typical North African culture equivalent to the later paleolithic of Europe. Rock drawings from Algeria resembles those in later French and Spanish caves."

"Of the physical characteristics of the Euro-African man we learn more at the present European sites than from the ill explored areas further south." *Cambridge Ancient History,* Vol. 1, page 49, "The other type distinctly Negroid is best represented by skeleton from the Grimaldi Cave near Mentone. There can be little doubt of its African origin and there are two indications of such African types in Europe. A Pygmy breed of somewhat Negroid appearance—and the well marked Steatopygy which characterizes Negroid Bushmen and Hottentots of South Africa of some other Negroid breed further north and is represented in European drawings and sculpture of female figures. Aurignacian times to the Neolithic Art of Malta."

Jean Finot in his book *Race Prejudice*, page 99, says: Let us remember according Guiseppi Sergi and Professor Briton: "The white race the ethnophical pride of Europe is only a direct fruit of the Negro race.

The Euro-African established in Europe from time immemorial and who came up from North Africa. A consistory is given to this theory by the fact that a number of bones said to be Negroid have been discovered in different parts of Europe.

Sir Harry H. Johnston gives us the most direct and striking evidence to this fact of his articles published in the volume: *Inter-Racial Problems*, page 330. Sir Harry says: "The actual fact that many thousand years ago, a Negroid race had penetrated Europe through Italy and France, leaving traces at the present day in the people of Southern Italy, Sicily, Sardinia, Southern and Western France and even in the United Kingdom of Great Britain and Ireland."

There are even at the present time some examples of the Kelto-Iberian people of western Scotland,

[86]

southern and western Wales of distinctly Negroid aspect.

The Ancient Picts of Scotland is said to be the ancestor of the small black race in Scotland. Cambridge *Ancient History*, Vol. 2, page 34.

G. Frederick Wright's Book: *The Origin and Antiquity of Man*, page 119, says: "To the theory that the original inhabitants of Europe were a long headed dark skinned race, affiliated with Negroes, additional likelihood is given by careful study of the existing races of Russia and Scandinavia."

Recent investigation shows that the Slavs are a broad headed race, but the Baltic Sea is bordered by a long headed race on both sides. Measurements of skeletons which are found in burrows and tumuli in Denmark, Sweden and Russia show that the prehistoric people who erected them belong also to a long headed race.

The term Dolichocephalic means long heads. This is the race that came from Africa and settled in Europe during prehistoric times. The Negro is classified as having a dalilichephalic skull-long head.

William Z. Ripley in his book *Races of Europe*, page 436, says: The discoveries of abundant prehistoric remains all over Europe particularly France. These with one accord tended to show that European Aborigines of the Stone Age were not Mongoloid like the Lapps, after all but the exact opposite. In every detail they resembled rather the dalilichachapic Negroes of Africa.

The Ancient Iberians also inhabited all Europe from Spain to the Caucasus Mountains. The New

[87]

Larned History says Vol. 5, 4193 "The Iberian inhabited the greater part of the Mowern province of Georgia, the British Isle, Germany and Denmark."

It is said that two great races inhabited Europe during the prehistoric period. First the Cro-Magnon Race and later the Iberian people. It would now be of interest to know definitely about these two races and what relation one bore to the other.

Now Paul Radin takes us back one hundred thousand years in Geological History or the Records of the Rocks to the Old Stone Age when he says in his book called *Racial Myths,* page 55, "But when we turn to the very bases of all civilization, the achievements made during the Old Stone Age, beginning a hundred thousand years ago we cannot make out a good case for any of the ancestors of our present races. . . . If a case can be made for any of them it is the Negro, for the white race all we can say or possibly hope is that they are in some degree descended from the Cro-Magnon Race which flourished in Europe from twenty thousand to ten thousand years ago."

Now who were the Cro-Magnon? Isaac Taylor in his book *The Origin of the Aryan,* page 96, says: "The importance of the skeleton of the Cro-Magnon type is that in stature, prognasitum, . . . they exhibit approximation to the Negro type more than any other which have been found in Europe".

Sir Arthur Keith says: "That is no good reason for separating the so-called Negroids from other members of the Cro-Magnon stock, they have essentially the same features of that stock".

[88]

Now if the Cro-Magnon Race flourished in Europe from twenty-five thousand to ten thousand years ago, the Iberian Race is said to have overran Europe and threatened to conquer the world five thousand years ago between the two definite periods. It would be logical for me to agree with Isaac Taylor in his book *The Origin of the Aryan,* page 101, when he says: The Iberian descended from the Cro-Magnon Race. If as is contended by Broca and Quatrefages the Cro-Magnon people exhibit a remote ancestral type of the Iberian Race. The question of the ultimate origin the Iberian would be greatly simplified.

Broca considers their resemblance of the Berbers that migrated into Europe from Africa of the Guanche and Berber skulls to those of the Ancient Egyptian allies them to the Great Hamitic stock, the Cro-Magnon skeleton forming a link between the Berber and the Negroes.

We will conclude this chapter with the words of Sir Harry Johnston's article in *Inter-Racial Problems,* page 336, what he says about the Negro that he may die out in Asia but in Africa and in America he has a very important part to play and he may even permeate the life of Europe in the coming centuries.

8

Negroes in Ancient America

It is now an established theory and a popular belief that the ancestors of the American Indians came to America from Asia and probably crossed from the Asiatic mainland by the way of the Alleutian Island across the Bering Strait, a very narrow passage of water separating the northwestern part of the North American continent from Asia. The argument is very logical from a geographical point of view but the monuments and the ancient culture which has been discovered and disclosed in later years in such countries as Mexico, Central and South America, definitely show that the ancient forefathers of the American Indians were of African origin not Asiatic.

A glance at a map of the South Atlantic would seem to indicate that the Eastern Coast of Brazil and the western part of Africa were once joined together as one plot of land, but rent asunder during the geographical re-arrangement caused by the flood "In the days of Noah". Brighane in his book *Shadow of the Atlantis,* page 71, says: "that the eastern shore of Brazil and the western shore of Africa, if it were possible for these two continents to be reconnected, would fit perfectly". Brighane qoutes "Dr. A. Wagner as saying that the separation of South America and South Africa took place between thirty and forty million years ago".

Be that as it may regardless of the chronology of the event as to when the separation took place, my contention is the two continents were once connected as one continent before the flood. The geographical outline of the western portion of Africa and the coast of Brazil, if these two continents were joined back together, they would fit perfectly. South America is nothing more or less than the Lost Atlantis or that portion of Africa that was separated during the flood. The generic definition of Atlantis is evolved from such terms as Adlan or At-lan—the land of Adam. Adlantis or Atlantis or Atlantic—Adam's land divided by water. Adam was once a very wealthy man, "The watery worlds were all his own, and also all the solid ground.

So this prehistoric Continent before the flood was peopled by a race what political writers today would brand as "Negroes" who first inhabited South America, Central America and Mexico. Mexico has been often called the "American Egypt". The people of Mexico were called Aztecs and their country Aztlan which is only a slight variation of Atlantis which means identical. The children of Adam are a prehistoric Ethiopian race. These Negro tribes still found in South America are the Aborigines of the Continent and the ancestors of the American Indians of North and South America and the West India Islands.

South and Central America was peopled before North America just as Africa and Southern Asia was the first habitation of man long before the migration to Europe and Northern Asia, for many centuries in the life of early man, Europe, Northern Asia and North America was under a sheet of ice.

If the ancestors of the American Indians had come to America by the way of Alaska or in other words from Asia, they would have left the blue print of the establishment of their culture in Eastern Asia and too they would not have come down through the long length and breadth of the Continent of North America without building a pyramid or spinx or some temple or palace that would have been similar to the ones that are now found in Mexico, Central and South America.

Lost Histories of America
W. S. Blackett—Page 276-277 says:

"The Inca (Peru) and his institutions may have been unknown in Asia and Europe from Plato to Columbus; but there are ocular demonstrations from the monuments of antiquity. The Inca and his customs were known in ancient Ethiopian and Babylonia. Further evidence are given from an Ethiopian picture which was taken from a Peruvian scene on the rules that decide such questions. Peruvian picture is a simple natural scene. It is the Inca in his temple before the Sun God, while in the Ethiopian design there are ghosts bringing offerings to him. Both Nations, the Incas of Peru, South America, and the Ethiopian of Africa were worshippers of the Sun God."

NEGROES IN AMERICA TWENTY THOUSAND YEARS AGO

The modern historians tells us that the Negroes were first brought to America over three hundred years ago, to work as slaves. But further research have found that Negroes inhabited America something like twenty thousand years ago, and further shows that they were the first Americans and not the Mongolians crossing the narrow passage of water at the Bering Strait to Alaska. The Negroes were always here, they were Aborigines of the continents of the Americas and also the ancestors of the American Indians.

They did not come by migration, they were on the continent of South America when it was rent asunder from Africa at the time of the flood.

A. Brighane in his book *The Shadow of the Atlantis,* page 140, says—"the fact that the existence of Black Races among the inhabitants of the Lost Continents mentioned in the Codex Popul-Vuh (the Sacred Book of the Mayas) is of greatest interest. Hitherto, ethnologist imagine that Negroids appeared in the new world during our own epoch, but most recent researches, demonstrates that they came to America in a period very remote."

Mr. Brighane further states that "It is not impossible that in the present African Black populations, the decendants of some Atlantean Black-skinned tribes still exist".

Brighane supports his argument with such noted authors as Quatrefages, La Plongeon and Bancroft of whom he says have proved that certain Aborigines Negro tribes have inhabited America not so very

[93]

long ago. Some statues of Gods in Central America possess Negro features, and certain historic monuments there undoubtedly represent Negroes. He further asserts that such statues in Teotihuacan, in Palenque, and a gigantic Negro statue carved in granite near the Mexican volcano of Taxila.

"I have seen a statuette of a Negro in the Archaeological collection of Mr. Ernesto France in Quinto (Ecuadori). According to the opinion of logical archaelogical the statuette is at least twenty thousand years old. But in a very remote time Negroes or Negroids were numberous in the new world."

A. De Quatrefages, professor of Anthropolgy of the Museum of Natural History at the University of Paris, says in his book, *Human Species,* page 200, Black population have been found in America. Such are the Charruas of Brazil, the Black Carabees of Saint Vincent in the Gulf of Mexico, the Jamissi of Florida, the dark complexion Californian; such again is the tribe which Balbo saw, some representatives in his passage of the Isthmus of Darien in 1513—that these were true Negroes. There is a tribe of Negroes in Brazil that is called Sarmaccas, and some consider these Negroes to be an Antochthonous American tribe. They even have their own language.

Brighane's *Shadow of the Atlantis,* page 38, says: "The Caro tribes in Kansas and the Californians are very dark."

Professor Retzuis considers that all primeval dolichephalic tribes of America in America are very related to the Guanches of the Canary Islands and to the races which inhabit the shores of Africa.

Donnelly in his book *Atlantis,* page 175, speaks of the Gigantic Negro Statue at the palace near Taxilo and says of the features that the "Face was strongly Ethiopian" but Mr. Donnelly strives to make it appear this Negro statue was a slave because Negroes he says were never a sea faring race. But he falls ridiculously short of the goal of his argument. Monuments are not erected to slaves, but only to gods, kings and heroes.

The duck bill Indian women in the Jungles of South America stretched their lips when young in the very similar custom to the Duck bill women of Ubanga tribes in Africa.

John F. Farris in his book *Seeing South America,* page 44, says: "The Jungle Indians have a method of rapid communication with one another that is like that described by travelers in parts of Africa, signals are given by beating on a six foot tree hollowed by fire, a rude drum whose voice proves affective, those who would hear the message must place their ears on a like drum, the radio of the jungle can do its work".

This goes to show that the American Indians are the direct descendents of African Negroes, the Africans have had their radio drum for ages. Their language or dialect resembles that of the Gold Coast of West Africa.

Pritchord in his book *The Natural History of Man,* pages 410-411, quotes LaPerouse on Black Indians and compares them to the Negroes in the West Indies he says "The color of these Indians which is the same as that of Negroes, a variety of circumstances and indeed everything that we observed presented the appearance of a Plantation in the Island of St. Domingo". He continues "It seems from this description that color is not only circumstance in which the Californian makes an approximation to the character of person prevalent in some other tropical countries (West Africa, and the Island of the Pacific) . . . ."

From an editorial in the *Ethiopian World—* Monthly Publication. "African Negroes Discovered America Before Columbus," November, 1940:

The Black Race comes down from a civilization that it need not be ashamed. We are not an inferior Race, but it is a misguided Race, miseducated and misinformed which gives it the inferiority complex.

The Black Race has one of the richest heritages in history—Recent exploration and documents of neglected history has thrown much light upon the master achievements of the African Negro which is a fact that reads stranger than fiction. The book *Africa and the Discovery of America* by Leo Weiner, a Harvard Professor who speaks more than twenty different languages and dialects—the Book was reviewed in the *World's Work* magazine and *Literary Digest* and other leading periodicals say that Columbus found that America had been discovered by Negroes on second arrival in this hemisphere, that he also found Negros living in South America, they told him that their ancestors came here from the South East (Africa) and carried some of them back to Spain with the Indians and presented them to the court of the King and Queen of Spain.

[96]

Professor Weiner also claims that Sweet Potatoes, Peanuts and tobacco were brought from Africa by the Negroes who taught the Indians how to cultivate them. Another book titled the *Hand of God in History*, sustains these claims that the African Negroes discovered America before Columbus, but the Spanish being eager for honor, kept it a secret. The Ancient Ruins of the Mayan Civilization, the Pyramids of Mexico, are identically the same as found in Egypt. The monuments pure Negro features thick lips and flat nose. These monuments were not slave monuments, they do not erect monument to slaves.

Ancient Egyptians were African Negroes. We know that modern customs have claimed the Egyptians to belong to most any other race than Negro. But we have facts to prove that they were one hundred per cent pure African Blacks. The ancient Egyptians descended from the Ethiopians and built the first world's greatest empire. The Egyptians claimed their descent was from Ethiopia—a branch of the Ethiopian race.

Heeren's *Historical Research on African Nations* says: "Thebes as well as the states in general upper Egypt are called in proper annals of Priest. Colonies from Meroe in Ethiopia and at Thebes Service of Jupiter Ammon whose temples were common centers of the State, gives of itself a striking proof that such was the case. The other cities of Egypt, likewise derive their descent, directly or indirectly from Ethiopia. Robert Hartman Scientist and historian says: "That the Egyptians were the genuine children of Africa, who stood indisputable

physical relation with the races of the Continent."
Africa has written her history in monuments. The
Sphinx has the face of an African woman, thick lips
and broad nostrils which show to all the world, that
a Black Pharaoh ruled the Delta at the time of its
Erection.

9

Ethiopia in the Role of International Politics

The fifteenth century marked the beginning of the most adventurous period in European history. It saw the downfall of the Moorish Kingdom in Spain. It witnessed the ascendancy of King Ferdinand and Queen Isabella to the throne of Spain which ushered in the dawn of the Golden Days of the house of Castille.

Spain and Portugal were at that time the leading sea powers in Europe. The Spanish Armada was the mistress of the ocean. The Spanish and Portuguese Princes and Noblemen sailed the Seven Seas, circumnavigate the globe, explored unknown wilds and with the Keys of Adventure unlocked the doors of twin Continents and presented the Americas to Europe on a silver platter.

Then the jealousy and rivalry between European nations over colonial claims had their beginning, until it climaxed into the present world crisis.

King Francis of France said that he would like to see the "clause in Adam's will that gave to Spain and Portugal the right to divide the world between themselves". The first penetration of Africa by European nations of modern times had its beginning during this period.

Christopher Da Gama, the half-brother of Vassa Da Gama, a Portuguese nobleman with four hundred soldiers aided the Abyssinian in repelling and driving back the Mohamendan invasion. But Christopher Da Gama had more interest in gold finding than he had in religion.

Ethiopia was the first key point to European pentration in Africa, and today Ethiopia has become the sacred trust of African redemption, and the peace of the world, when the Black Empire was crucified for the sake of World's Democracy, but she has "risen again". The Ethiopian Empire was first known to European Nations as Abyssinia— An Ethiopian word "Alberogran", meaning mountainous or Lofty Plain. The term Abyssinia has no references to mixed races as some writers have asserted. The original name of Ethiopia was restored by his Majesty Haile Selassie.

From time immemorial Ethiopia has played an important part and often the leading role in the affairs of the world. The Bible as well as Secular history confirms this fact.

The Ethiopian armies stormed the walls of Mecca during the fifth century A.D. and had her troop been supported by an ally, Mohammedan religion would have been crushed in its cradle. While the Mohammedan succeeded in conquering and converting nearly one-third of the native African population, Ethiopia stood firm "As a Christian Island in a Pagan Sea". Modern Ethiopia was first brought into notice in European Politics during the reign of "King Theodore" when the Lion of the tribe of Judah crossed swords with the British Lion in British-Abyssinian War 1867-8. The event which provoked the crisis it is said was Queen Victoria's refusal to recognize the Ethopian Ambassador at the Court of St. James in Native costume, King Theodore retaliated by imprisoning the British Consul and the British missionaries then in Abyssinia.

The British government sent out an expedition under the command of Lord Napies this war ended in the defeat of Theodore armies, the British subjects were released and King Theodore committed suicide. Napier defeated the Ethiopians in the battile of Magdala for this victory he was knighted as Napier of Magdala: But this victory in Ethiopia did not create any mass interest for colonial design on Africa, beyond the equator it was still looked upon as a Dark Continent, while European nations still dreamed and planned to regain their former possession in the Americas, France and England especially had been former colonial rivals, but their chances soon vanished in the event that followed our Civil War.

The war between the States during the decade of the 60's with such battles as Gettysburg and Richmond which resulted in the downfall of the Southern Confederacy. This war enabled President Lincoln to consolidate the States of the Union with a "Rebirth of Freedom." Following these events was the Maxmillan plot to seize Mexico, he was jailed and shot, then later, England was made to pay indemnity for giving aid to Southern Confederacy. America put teeth in the Monroe Doctrine which put to flight the European colonial policy to "divide and conquer" on the Western Hemisphere then and not until then did Europe look for New Worlds to conquer and exploit. Although they had made some adventure in the tropical areas but only with minor interest to that which they had manifested in the Americas.

During this Colonial Dilemma, Henry M. Stanley made his return from an expedition in Africa where he had gone in search for Livingston the Scottish Missionary. Stanley succeeded in finding Livingston but he had done more, Stanley discovered Africa's economical possibilities and advertised it to the anxious colonial monsters of Europe. Stanley did for Africa what Americus Vespusci did for the New World, America, which bears his name, while Christopher Columbus discovered America, Americus Vespusci sold the value of the discovery to the European World.

The same was never the less true of Africa, David Livingston, the devout Missionary was the first trail-blazer to bear the Standard of the Cross to the benighted regions and gave his life for Africa's redemption, but the Stanley expedition sold the idea of commercial exploitation to the European nations which has reduced the "Black Continent" to exploitation and slavery, that is unparalleled in the annals of history. The foremost champion of this colonial movement was Count Otto Von Bismark the Iron Chancellor of the German Empire who assembled the representatives from the leading nations of Europe to a session that is known as the Conference of Berlin (1884). The aim and purpose of the Berlin Conference was to have an understanding among the powers in the petitioning of the entire African Continent among European nations who desired a share of the spoil.

The Iron Chancellor thought that such an agreement would avoid the conflict that the nations of Europe had experienced in their colonial scramble in America. King Leopold had already held similar meetings in Brussels but they did not exert the volume of pressure as did the Conference in Berlin. The nations of Europe divided the Continent of Africa among themselves, their concession became colonial plantation for the Sole purpose of exploiting the natural resources at the expense of Native forced labor and they subjugated the passive innocent people to state of slavery which would make the bondage of the Negro in our southern States before the Civil War, look like a democracy in comparison.

The system of Slavery in America was bad enough but it was by far more human than Europe's rape of Africa: the Slaves of America were better protected because of the master's investment, but in Africa the master did not have to buy them and the natives there were looked on as a menace to white settlers. For fear of uprising they were often treated with the most extreme cruelties and subjected to untold horrors. Leopold's atrocities in the Congo Free States in 1900, his brutal punishment of innocent natives on the rubber plantation, is one of the blackest chapters in the history of civilized man.

The British in South and East Africa, the French in Morocco, the Italian in Ethiopia all have been guilty before God for the savage and brutal outrage inflicted upon defenseless Africa for three hundred years. While we deplore the bombing of the Capitals of Europe and such buildings as Saint Paul in London, and Rome the Holy City. We forget that Africa is Holy Ground, crucified and enslaved for the past three centuries, in Africa "every stone would make an altar for a prayer and every rock could be a seat for a prophet."

The opening up of the African Continent did not influence mass imigration as it did in the discovery of the America. Africa has never been inviting to the White Race as a homeland, it has been dreaded and looked upon as a "White Man's Grave Yard," as the major portion of its Continental confines are within the tropical belt with the exception of the Southern and Eastern fringe, the Continent where the climate is somewhat temperate and along the high plateau of the Eastern sections toward the Red Sea and Indian Ocean and even there it is hot enough.

Under the European colonial policy the false term "Sacred Trust," and "Stewardship" for backward natives these European monsters have bled the Black Continent white. The surplus population of Europe migrated to America only to meet, in the Northern and Eastern industrial centers, a keen competition of Negro labor coming from the South where riots are so common until it is not news.

From 1869 to 1900 thirteen million eight hundred and seventy-five thousand imigrants came from

Europe to America and today there are approximately thirty million persons of European descent in United States either foreign born or born of foreign parents.

There are more than seven times as many European imigrants in New York City than all the whites who have imigrated to Africa within the past fifty years, nine-tenths of all of Europe's imigrants come to America and yet three-fourths of territory controlled by Europe is in Africa.

The climate of North America is similar to that of Europe plus the advantage given Europeans in various industries protected from the competition of Negro labor and defended by "Sit down Strikes." But in Africa there is no demand for white labor. Native cheap labor is a monopoly. The same was true in the southern States of America, before the Civil War, where slave labor was a serious handicap to the poor whites of the South and its reaction was a stumbling block to the free states of the North, this was largely the cause of the Civil War. The population of the South at that time was about nine million persons: there were three million white who did not own slaves, four million five hundred thousand slaves and two million and a half slave owners. The Big Southern plantations averaged from two thousand to three thousand acres and there were plantations that contained as much as ten thousand acres of cotton land.

When President Abraham Lincoln struck down the monster of Slavery, bruised and wounded but not dead, his system retreated to Africa, where he Shackled a Continent and enslaved a Black world.

The southern slave plantations were but a blue print in comparison for it served as the pattern on which they built on a vast scale. The southern plantation was from two to ten thousand acres but in Africa with a population of 2,680,000 backed by their Home Government they controlled the destiny of 400,000,000 Negroes and Negroid and over forty times the size of their colonial home Governments in Europe. There respective areas are as follows:

	Square miles
British Africa	3,485,570
French Africa	4,285,200
Belgian Congo	947,200
Portuguese Africa	799,200
Italian Africa	774,500
Spanish Africa	103,300
Negro Africa (Ethiopia)	350,000
Liberia	36,800

The above figures give some conception of the colonial States of Africa compared to the territorial possession of the Black Race in his home Continent. Europe controlled nearly eleven million square miles, leaving less than a half a million square miles under the control of the Black Race.

These European nations at the close of Nineteenth Century had succeeded in partitioning the entire African Continent, with the exceptions of Liberia and Ethiopia and even their independence was constantly threatened.

Liberia being an American colony, the good influence of the United States served to protect its existence. Ethiopia being a Christian Nation and a country of deep range mountain and jungles which seemed a natural fortress for its protection, the power at first sought other methods to subjugate her rather than by armed force. They also realized that any defeat of a Colonial Power by an African nation might influence tribal revolt throughout Africa and change the complex of their colonial programme.

The powers gradually encircled Ethiopia in the acquirement of territory in East Africa known as the British, French and Italian Somaliland which surrounded the country, cutting her off from the Sea, making her land-locked Empire in order to reduce her to their zones of influence, thus making Ethiopia a Segregated Nation. Italy made the first venture for the conquest of the Black country, sent an expeditionary force 1895-6 to invade and overthrow the Menelik Regime and make Ethiopia an Italian province this event was known as the Italo-Abyssinia War. The Italian armies were disastrously defeated by the Ethiopians under the command of King Menelik, the scene at the Battle Adowa. This defeat of Italy by this Black Nation, caused much concern among the colonial powers, especially Britain and France. It caused them to re-affirm the act of Berlin to "stand jointly together in Africa, with one accord and understanding.

England, France and Italy then formed a partnership among themselves known as the Tripatite Treaty to divide Ethiopia into three zones of influence this treaty was formed in 1906. It gave England the right of control over the Lake Tana Basin which is the head water of the Blue Nile, to irrigate the cotton lands of Soudan and Egypt, the

French concession demanded the right of way for a Railroad to run from Addis Abba, the Ethiopian Capitol through the French Somaliland to the Red Sea port at Djibouti, with one member of each of the respective nations including Ethiopia as a Board of Control. Italy was granted the right to build another road from the Red Sea port in Eritrea, to run through Northern Ethiopia to connect the Somaliland province, they also formulated a power agreement to respect the integrity of Ethiopia. But after signing the Tripartite Treaty each of the three powers became jealous and suspicious of the other, the treaty specified that all transaction with Ethiopia should be done jointly with all parties of the agreement present, but France double-crossed England and Italy and signed a separate agreement with Ethiopia to build this road which is known as the Franco Ethiopian Railroad, it completed in 1917 the Franco-Ethiopian agreement made Ethiopia an equal partner with France instead of a victim to the three power aggression.

This single handed deal by France created a feeling of distrust in the minds of her British and Italian partners, French diplomats realized the possibilities and reactions that would follow this Franco-Ethiopian deal, negotiated Ethiopia's membership in 1922, into the League of Nations to protect her from British-Italian encroachment.

Haile Selassie then Prince Regent of Ethiopia, known then as Ras Tafaria, arrived in Paris, enroute to Geneva. When the French liner docked at Brest and the Ethiopian Prince stepped from the gangplank on French soil, the government fired 21 cannon as a Military Salute, while the mass crowds shouted with loud applause: "long live Ethiopia."

France again in 1923 projected another Railroad Scheme, known as the Trans-Sahara, which was routed from the Mediterranean Sea coast at Algiers through Tunisia across the Sahara to the Black belt of African colonies with connecting links to Lake Chad and the Belgian Congo with further plans for extending it through the former German East African Territory, known as the Trans-African Railroad with engines designed to run by electricity and petroleum because of the lack of water in the desert. Such a scheme if carried out would have been a keen competitor to the British zone of influence. This proposed French Line would have given a greater commercial service, for trade and travel to the direct markets of Europe, than the British Capetown to Cairo, route by the way of Suez. The Trans-Sahara trains would have been limited, in event of war, to military purpose for the transportation of colonial troops, to European battle fields. The French Black Empire in Africa created a grave concern to the British commonwealth of nations. It threatened the peace of Europe with the thunder heads of a Black Peril, endangered the Life Line of England's far flung Empire, through the Mediterranean and Red Sea, its main route to India and the East.

France had built up the most powerful black army that Europe had seen since the days of Hannibal, this vast colonial army including Algerian, Moroccan and Senegalese was estimated at two million troops. During the last World War, one hun-

dred and eighty-one thousand French Black troops
fought with honor on European and Asiatic battle-
fronts. This is when Europe discovered that France
had drilled the "Blackman White and woke up
Pharaoh." The French occupation of the Rhine
with African troops was met with stern protest
from the German people, which enable the German
propaganda agents to win the sympathy of French
allies.

During the two stormy decades that followed the
close of the first World War, Germany laid its plans
to divide and conquer, their propaganda agents
were able to pack water on both shoulders and carry
a bucket on their heads. They first organized a system of racial hate toward the Jews and with a little
effort they become high powered salesmen in making the sons of Abraham their first victims by
preaching that the Jewish monopoly of business,
that the house Rothschild and other Jewish banking
firms, control the money markets of Europe and the
world. This propaganda did not only gain a foot-
hold in Europe but it also made converts in
America.

Their second effort of propaganda was to divide
England from France, it had its "The Negro in the
Wood Pile," by claiming that France was bas-
tardizing Europe with Negro blood and the French
population was increasingly Negroid that France
had no color line and that her women and girls
freely mingled with her black troops and often married them, these German propagandists pointed out
that the French Black troops were a menace to the
peace of Europe and direct threat to Nordic Su-

premacy—this doctrine of Negro equality in France and French Black colonial menace found a ready audience in Europe and had a profound effect on the British colonial interest.

Propaganda number three, the next turn was Italy's where they played another but most successful role and reached a key point in turning the tide of European politics, they reprimanded Italy, for breaking her pledge with Germany during the late World War, as a member of the triple alliance. When Italy broke from the Central Powers and drew her sword in defense of the Allies, that the Allies double-crossed Italy at the Conference of Versailles and her Prime Minister returned home without Italy's share of the spoils of war. Because of this they was able to influence Mussolini to become an ally to Nazi Germany, for Italy too, nourish a grievance for the want of colonies.

Hitler was to reclaim the former German African colonies and Mussolini would receive the territory he desired, this is why Hitler was able to seize Austria without firing a gun, Italy remaining neutral at Brenner Pass.

These strange incidents in European politics baffle the diplomacy of the British Statesmen, with a French Colonial menace in Africa on one hand and German-Italian aggression on the other, all the while France remained an ally to England in Europe. But Britain needed an ally in Africa to augment French expansion, that in event of war with France, to keep the British colonies from being exposed to the wrath of the French colonial troops. England and France had been colonial rivals for the two hundred years. They fought each other on contested colonial grounds wherever they could carry a gun from the plains of Abraham in Canada, where the British and French generals in command both fell mortally wounded on the eve of victory and defeat. France fought England here in the colonial days of America with the Indian Chief Tecumseh and his red braves as an ally in the French Army. She fought England in Egypt in the days of Napoleon under the shadows of the pyramids, the honorable deeds of Lord Nelson in the Battle of the Nile, writes one of the sublimest chapters in British military annals. France fought England in India, and was defeated by the British armies under Commander Clive a victory that knighted him as Clive of India.

Lafayette, a French nobleman, volunteered his service to General George Washington to serve as Major General in the Revolutionary War without pay. This time France fought with America against England not because of the love she had for America, but for revenge. These experiences caused England to distrust France in Africa. This critical situation gave Mussolini an opportunity to play a double role in European politics with both, he had a common objective with each of his partners.

Italy linked its cause with Germany, in her effort to regain her lost African colonies, Mussolini sought expansion in East Africa, with Ethiopia as his first goal, both Germany and Italy nursed grievances against France and England. England not being able to trust France in Africa and in order to appease Mussolini to prevent his lining up with

Hitler, signed a pact in 1925 with Italy known as an Anglo-Italian agreement, bringing pressure on France for her violation of Tripartite Treaty when France built the Franco-Ethiopian Railroad which virtually made Ethiopia a French ally. This Anglo-Italian agreement was a substitute to the Tripartite Treaty and held to the same rights and claims as the former three power agreement 1906 to divide Ethiopia into three zones of influence which never had been carried out.

The Ethiopian representatives protested against this aggressive move before the League of Nation at Geneva and the powers backed down for the time being, the Ethiopian King realizing his country was surrounded both by land and sea and threatened with dismemberment made it a fertile field for Japanese penetration. The Japanese propaganda against Western Imperialism found a ready audience in East Africa and Ethiopia becoming the key to Japanese penetration.

The Japanese came with a diplomacy like "wolves in sheep clothing" preaching the doctrine of Racial hate, against the white race in Africa, as Hitler was doing against the Jews in Europe. The Japanese entered Ethiopia posing as benefactor of all colored races they came with such high pressure Salesmanship enabling these so-called "sons of Heaven" to secure concession for nearly nine million acres of land without cost, for the production of coffee, cotton and colonization by Japanese Nationals. The two governments agreed for the intermarriage between the Ethiopian and Japanese colonist. The

[113]

Ethiopian-Japanese agreement enabled Japan to gain eighty per cent of Ethiopia textile trade.

A Japanese nobleman's daughter became engaged to an Ethiopian Prince, the prospective bride remarked that she thought it an honor to marry an Ethiopian Prince because "The Ethiopians were a fighting race." This royal engagement was protested by Rome through the Italian embassy at Tokio with a threatening diplomatic breach between Italy and Japan because it threatened the Italian zone of influence, the wedding was postponed and for its further activities we have no press record.

A press dispatch from Tokio a few years ago stated that Japan included East Africa in her zone of new order in Asia. The *New York Times* quoting a Japanese newspaper *Nichi-Nichi* in saying the "New order includes the emancipation of the people of East Africa and the South Sea from European aggression."

The Japanese penetration in East Africa complicated more the already confused system of Europe's colonial diplomacy; the British Empire found itself at the crossroad with another German menace in Europe, French rivalry in equatorial Africa, the Gandhi passive but National movement in India, the Japanese New Order in Eastern Asia and Italy's dissatisfaction of being deprived of her share of colonies at the conference of Versailles. During these stirring events France found herself on the spot, she sought to influence Italy from the Germans and also to double check the Anglo-Italian agreements. France thought the time ripe for her

The Reception to Haile Selassie Upon His Return to the Throne of Ethiopia

The Ethiopian Church at Axum, the Ancient Capital of Ethiopia, in the Days of the Queen of Sheba

The Ethiopian Children

to gain Mussolini's favor. She gave Italy 44,500,000 square miles of territory in East Africa and then sold Mussolini three thousand shares in the Franco-Ethiopian railroad.

The Japanese new order included the emancipation of the people of East Africa and the South Sea from European aggression but later Japan deserted and double-crossed Ethiopia in her hour of gravest peril by becoming a partner to the Berlin-Rome Axis and also a partner for the destruction of a nation which she had pledged to defend. War clouds of the approaching crisis swung like a black fog fell over European skies, the vast volume of critical moments baffled the minds of European Chancellors and Diplomats. England did not want Ethiopia dismembered to become a part of the Italian Empire, it would jeopardize the British life line to the East and would handicap her control of the Delta of the Nile, her main artery on the continents. The British respected the integrity of Ethiopia because of its ancient culture and Christian tradition and was willing for Italy to have a zone of influence, to build a railway to connect up her colonies, but no further penetration for it would threaten British interest.

The Anglo-Italian agreement and the proposal offered by England was not enough for Mussolini. The 44,500 square miles of territory and the partnership in the Franco-Ethiopian rail ceded to Mussolini, all was too little and too late, Italy cast her lot with Germany and Mussolini assumed the role of a modern Caesar "The die was cast" he mobilized his Black Shirt Legions to meet the Black men of Ethiopia.

The Italian dictator like Sciopio Africanus who advocated the overthrow of Carthage the Black Empire of North Africa, with the Slogan (Carthage must be destroyed), Benito Africanus had the same aim and purpose of his ancient predecessor, Mussolini vowed that "Ethiopia must be destroyed." He defied the former partners and sent his troop ships through the Suez Canal and fired on the ancient Empire, of the Queen of Sheba, a Black Empire that was backed by the tradition of fifty centuries of culture; while fifty-two nations, the members of the League, like Pontius Pilate washed their hands and beheld the crucifixion of Ethiopia upon the cross of world's Democracy, but it was not conquered.

The League of Nations is not dead, just crushed to earth and it will rise again to live ever after as "the Parliament of Man and the Federation of the World." The League of Nations was designed for a Super international government, President Woodrow Wilson its founder had the Soul of George Washington and the Spirit of Abraham Lincoln combined; like Washington he founded the United States of the World, with its capitol at Geneva; like Lincoln he proclaimed the doctrines of self determination for all races and nations, in this he changed the psychology of international politics. The Spirit of Nationalism swept across the world like wild fire in a dry forest, and all nations saw the solution of their problem in the light of self determination.

The breaking up of the League was similar, very much similar, to that of the United States in 1861, when South Carolina seceded from the Union and fired on Fort Sumpter, that incited the Civil War which was caused by the enslavement of the African people; so it is today the cause of the present crisis in Europe and the world. The enslavement and exploitation of the African continent by European nations, which has for three hundred years preyed upon the innocent people of the Ethiopian race who h is now stretched out their hands to God. The day of Europe's reckoning has come and this war is an International Civil War, for world Democracy, as Lincoln once said that America "can not exist half slave and half free" the same is nevertheless true with the world. Ethiopia was the direct cause of the war, when Italy violated the League Covenant and fired on the African Empire it made Addis Ababa another Fort Sumpter, the Black King riding a white horse ordered a returned fire whose shot was heard around the world, it disturbed the water of the Seven Seas from Gibraltar to Mandalay. The Mediterranean Sea became the Mason and Dixon Line of international politics, and her waters flow as vexed to the ocean as the Mississippi River did to the Sea in 1861; war flames leaped from Ethiopian highland and set ablaze the Capital of Europe and then swept across the Atlantic and it scorched the shores of South America when the German Admiral Graff Spee challenged the supremacy of the British Navy off the coast of Uruguay and when the Japanese Empire, supporting the Berlin-Rome Axis, in a daredevil attempt to break the Anglo-American solidarity fired on the outpost of United States fleet at Pearl Harbor, it set the world on fire and the

[117]

War assumed the role of Armageddon which has no parallel in the annals of military history. The summary of its vast volume can be better described in the epic lines of Homer.

Oh what heroes fired by thirst of flame.
Or urged by wrongs to Troy's destruction came.
To count them all demands a thousand tongues
A throat of brass and admantine lungs.

The Italo-Ethiopian war destroyed the very foundation of the world's security which was the sole cause of the present conflict, but there is one thing it did, it woke up race consciousness in the Negroes throughout the world more than anything has done in a thousand years, it was by far more intensifying than Marcus Garvey's dream of African Empire. The war electrified the race consciousness of the Black man from the jungles of Africa to the Black belts of Harlem, and Chicago and as far west as Kansas City and to the black belts of the south as far as Mobile, Ala., and demonstration by Negroes from the French colonies in Africa on the streets in Paris. The sleeping giant Africa was awakening from centuries of slumber. The natives in South Africa went on a strike and refused to unload an Italian ship that landed there. Several thousand Somaliland troops in East Africa, equipped with rifles and machine guns, deserted the Italian army and crossed the Somaliland-Ethiopian border and joined ranks with their Black Brothers in Ethiopia. The French African Negroes formed in vast numbers in Paris attempted to march on the Italian embassy in Paris, but were dispersed by the civil authorities but later in evening the Negroes formed another group and made demonstration in other sections of the city. Riots broke out in Harlem between Negroes and Italian, window glasses in Italian stores in Negro belts were smashed, four hundred Negroes battled policemen in the streets of New York. The same thing occurred between Negroes and Italians in Jersey City, Newark and Buffalo—an uprising among the natives in Kingston, St. Vincent, British West Indies, all because of the Ethiopian conflict.

The late Robert L. Van, the militant editor of the *Pittsburgh Courier,* sent Mr. J. A. Rogers as a reporter to the scene of the conflict, so as to give his readers first hand information direct from the Ethiopian fighting fronts.

Several thousand Negroes (American) volunteered their service to join the Ethiopian ranks to fight to save their traditional Fatherland their enlistment from the following cities were as follows: Chicago, 8,000; Detroit, 5,000; Kansas City, 1,500; Philadelphia, 1,500.

A Negro organization in Chicago launched a drive to raise six million dollars to aid the Ethiopian cause.

The Ethiopian volunteer movement became so momentous that the State Department in Washington enforced a law that was enacted in 1818, which makes it a penalty of one thousand dollars and three years in jail for any citizen of the United States to enlist in a foreign war. This law had a serious effect in checking the volunteer movement but it did not crush their zeal to aide the defense of Ethiopia,

[119]

other efforts were soon launched forward. The foremost among these were probably the Ethiopian World Federation (Inc.) with its headquarters in New York City, and other Ethiopian organizations sprang up in various cities of the United States, some for the defense of Ethiopia and others for the purpose of awakening race consciousness in the minds of the Americans.

A large group of Negroes in Mobile, Ala., organized a society known as the Friends of Ethiopia, launched a state wide drive for medical supplies and also the necessities for Ethiopian children. The Italo-Ethiopia war did more to unite the Negroes' interest in America towards Africa than any event which has occurred since his sojourn in America.

It did more than that, it also put to flight forever the false mis-classification of the Africans, the make-believe political propaganda, that the Ethiopians were not Negroes. This war showed and proved to the prejudiced writers on African anthropology that the Black races on both continents knew that they sprang from a common ancestor.

Almost every colored person that you may meet in America, whether they are educated or illiterate, know that Ethiopia is their ancient Fatherland. It was handed down through tradition from the slave days when Africans were brought to America, but African Life and history not being taught in school caused the black people in America to not know much about Ethiopia for several centuries, Ethiopia was known to moderns as Abyssinia which had much to do with confusing the traditional background of African Descendants in America,

When Haile Selassie ascended to the throne of Abyssinia in 1932 one of his most important official acts was his request to the Government of the civilized world to turn back the clocks of their geography four thousand years and restored the name of Ethiopia to its ancient heritage in history. The name within itself became a synonym of the Black Race throughout the world, even the tribes in the jungles of Africa and the Negroes of North and South America have a tradition of Ethiopia but not of Abyssinia. A colored woman in Portsmouth, Ohio, wept when the Radio dispatch announced the defeat of the Ethiopian armies. Had they said Abyssinians, the mass of the black race would not have been concerned. The name Abyssinia is not as familiar to the American Negro as Ethiopia. At the beginning of the war, King Selassie remarked: "Unhappy, if such conflict leads to a world struggle between the Black and White races, the very existence of humanity will be threatened." Before the Italo-Ethiopian war the Ethiopians had been classified as brunette, Caucasian, a Semite, or most anything else but a Negro, but the war caused the colonial powers to recognize them as Black people.

Haile Selassie's picture appeared in cartoon with regular African feature black with thick lips. The crisis brought about a split in the 1935 British cabinet election which was termed in London as "Nigger election." Mussolini with reference to Haile Selassie said that he would not remain in a league that was dominated by a "Nigger." "The Kinky Headed Haile Selassie, the last of the independent Negro Kings."

This war has done two great things much in the
favor of the Allies, it has restored the Negro Race
its Black King and England has restored his throne

THE VIGIL OF THE SPHINX

The features of the Massive Sphinx,
  Have a African Woman's face,
Nostrils broad, protruding lips,
  Of an ancient Negro race.
Her vigils through ages watch,
  Beneath Egyptian skies,
Still gaze across the desert sands,
  With her mysterious eyes.

Have seen the warlords pass away,
  And with the ages gone,
Those who went through seas of blood,
  And Slaughter to a throne.
The ancient sites and shattered ruins,
  Of Empires in the dust,
"Gone with the Winds," all their pride,
  Their vain and savage lust.

The scene is like the Desert's waste,
  Where the turtle dove laments,
Over Thebes' broken towers,
  And Memphis battlements.
The Sphinx reviewed King Cyrus Hordes,
  Alexander Phalanx braves;
And Ceaser's conquering legion,
  All alike are in their Graves.

She saw Napoleon's army,
  The words he uttered then,
From the tops of yonder pyramids,
  "Forty Centuries see you Men."
Lest you forget lightly tread,
  Where the warlike Pharaoh's sleep,
Lest you disturb the sacred dust,
  Where the Sphinx and her vigils keep.

Africa can never be conquered,
  For the Ghost of the Pharaoh are there,
And "Africa for the Africans",
  Are heard now everywhere.
Tut-Ankh-Amen come back from **Luxor,**
  Taharaqua lives again,
And the glories of a noble past,
  Inspire Ethiopian Men.

History repeats her circle roll,
  New Nation hood is born,
His Majesty Haile Selassie,
  Defends an ancient throne.

10

His Majesty Haile Selassie

Of the House of Solomon and the
Lion of the Tribe of Judah

Nearly four thousand years ago, the Patriarch Jacob said in his benediction on Judah that, "The Sceptre shall not depart from Judah; nor the lawgiver from between his feet, until Shiloh come," This prophecy is just as true today, as it was when it was spoken by the Seer of the Ancient East.

King Selassie I is the three hundred and thirtieth King of all the Kings of Ethiopia and the one hundred and thirtieth King of the Christian Empire.

According to the Ethiopian records and tradition, which goes back into the night of history, its first King was Aran, the thirty-fifth son of Adam, who ascended the Ethiopian throne four thousand and five hundred years before the birth of the Son of God.

The Solomon line comes down from the Queen of Sheba's son, Menelik I, whose father was King Solomon, but the interest that concerns us now is the part that is being played by the Black King in the greatest drama of World's Crisis that has ever met human intelligence.

The event marked its beginning in 1935, when Mussolini the "mad man" of Italy, sent his troop ships through the Suez Canal and violated the sanction of fifty-two nations and fired on Ethiopia. The crisis ushered the ancient Empire of the Queen of Sheba, into the role of international politics, and it made her Black King the property of History.

The King proclaimed one week of National Prayer before going into battle, Ethiopia, "stretched forth her hand to God," that her Sword might not return void of victory.

Haile Selassie was formerly known as Ras-Tafaria; he was Ras, (governor) of the Province of Harrar, and because of his culture and refined qualities he was called by his countrymen the "Golden Prince."

He sprang into prominence during the World War of 1916, as an Ally to England and France, he drew his Sword and defied the Moslem World and saved Africa and his Empire from Mohammedan invasion. When the armies of the allies and the central powers were locked in battle on the Western Fronts and the near East, the twenty-seven year old Crown Prince Lij Yassu, then ruler of Ethiopia was influenced by his father-in-law Mad Mullah, Mohammedan chief of British Somaliland, to lead an army against his own capital and compel his state official to denounce Christianity and adopt the Mohammedan Faith as a state religion, and then to organize an army of a half million soldiers and draw his Sword in the name of the Holy Prophet, and conquer the continent of Africa and build a vast Mohammedan Empire stretching from the Somaliland to British Nigeria. This sinister movement was checked by Haile Selassie, who lead a hundred thousand soldiers in battle against his royal cousin Lij Yassu. Lij Yassu was defeated, captured and imprisoned for life, but for the respect he had for his royal blood, Selassie handcuffed him with golden chains. Had Yassu not been checked in his attempt to excite the uprising of seventy-five million Mohammedans in Africa, for which his plot was planned, he probably would have changed the course of civilization. In checking this mad man of Ethiopia, Haile Selassie played the role of a "Defender of Democracy and a Soldier of the Cross."

Halie Selassie is the only one of the exiled Kings that has been able to return to his defeated country. He flew from London to Cairo, Egypt, August 1941. He put on his uniform in a bathroom in a Hotel in Cairo and with the vigor and spirit of a Texas cowboy, who would say "Give me back my boots and Saddle and let me roam the plains once more." He has returned to Ethiopia to lead an Army of two hundred and fifty thousand black soldiers, well equipped with British machine guns to chase the enemies of Ethiopia, to head them in for their Last Round Up."

The event is interesting, this bravery and strategy that has been displayed by the Ethiopians during the world's crisis, it has won the admiration of the world so much that some prejudiced writers have tried to take them out of the "Black Race" but even at that it was too late for a new creation, as a Jewish prophet once said that an "Ethiopian cannot change his skin."

When this great war is over and the nations of the earth will find themselves restored to the rank and file of a common Brotherhood, when democracy shall have a new birth of freedom, then crucified Ethiopia, and all of her Black sons, will rise and break the shackles that have bound them for centuries to take their places among the Nations of the Earth, then the sufferings of the Black Man, his patience, his passive nature, his song, his faith in his God will become the ideals of the Nations of the Earth when the "Drum tap is futile and barracks are exhausted."

11

The Insignificance of the Word Negro

The word Negro has done the Race more harm in America than any one known agency and has done more to impede his welfare and progress than any other given source.

It has become a "hiss" and byword in the United States. The word Negro is the most misused term in the world and also the most misleading.

There is no such race as a Negro, found on the pages of ancient history sacred or secular and I am only using the term Negro in this volume for the convenience of public usages. The word is not authentic when applied to Race. It is rather accommodative.

It is a Latin word meaning black and was formerly applied to the Africans living south of the Sahara by the Spaniards, but at that time the Spaniards were not so far wrong as the term has been converted to mean today. The Spanish word for Negro means "Black Moors" or Negro Moors.

The Spanish people have been in contact with the African nations from time immemorial, and they claimed that the so-called Negroes and Moors belong to the same race, only the former was darker because they were nearer the equator.

The word Negro Moor or Black Moor carried with it a greater respect than it does now. The Moors ruled and governed Spain for seven hundred and fifty years and had built an empire and culture the greatest Europe had seen since the fall of Greece and Rome.

The slave system of the Spanish and Portugese was a matter of cheap labor, but in the Teutonic North America slavery was cheap labor and also a matter of race fore-ordained for a "hewer of wood and a drawer of water."

The Spaniards had a higher respect for the black man from a racial standpoint than the Anglo-Saxon of North America; because of the former contact with them.

The term Moor and Negro-Moor had no meaning as to difference in races of Africa, than the term "blonde" and "brunette" would in Europe when referring to the Caucausian. Not as much.

Ordinarily, Spain is an off shoot of the African race, ancient Spain was known as an Iberian Ethiopia and the Spanish Peninsula is known to this day as the Iberian Peninsula.

Spain has been from ancient times invaded by black nations. She was first invaded by the Phoenician, an Asiatic black nation who gave to the world Hiram of Tyre who was a friend, and aid to Solomon in building the Temple at Jerusalem. She was afterward invaded and conquered by the Carthagians, a North African Nation in the days of Hannibal, one of the worlds greatest generals. She was also conquered by the Moors from North Africa. So there was never a question of color in its strictest sense in Spain.

She had a caste line, known as the Castillian, who descended from the Iberian Ethiopians but whenever this stock mixed or married with African mothers, their children were what would be termed in America "Creoles"; but in Spain, their children and the grandchildren would be termed as Spaniards.

The Spanish and Portugese were too proud to enslave their own blood though born without wedlock.

The Spanish and Portugese were in close relation to the Negro, at the time of the discovery of America. 40% of the people of Lisbon Portugal were Negroes, but since the term Negro has been converted to another meaning, it is used to misclassify the races of Africa to destroy the heritage of its history.

I have noticed the books written on Africa and about the Negro by some outstanding anthropologists and historians. Their books published by influential publishing companies, using such terms as "Negrellia, Negroes, Nigreto, Negeriti, Negroid, and also the word Nigger" has found its place in Webster Dictionary—such terms as above stated are misleading and both scientist and scholars abuse their intelligence when they try to build realities on such absurd expressions.

All of Africa belong to one Race, and that is the Ethiopian Race, while I admit there is some mix-

These Ethiopian Women Have Been Called to Arms. They Are Soldiers

The **Horses** of the Ethiopian Cavalrymen, are divided into three units, which serves as a Symbol or fulfilment of the prophecy of John's Seven Seals, the first Cavalrymen ride white horses, the second **bay** or chestnut horses, the third black horses. **Read** Revelations, the 6th Chapter.

ture of its population, but not one tenth as much as Europe.

Two-thirds of Europe is white in name only—while the Continent of Asia and its subordinate Pacific Island has three Races—The Mongolian; the Malays; and the Negroid.

The people of India as·a whole, are Asiatic Ethiopian. Nearly one third of the population of India has more or less distinctly Negroid features. But in Africa the population is ninety per cent African.

The scientist, Schmidt, in his volume *The Primitive Races of the Earth*, page 288, says: "the error was committed of referring nearly everything in Africa, both people and their culture to immigration from outside; admitting the African origin only to the Bushmen and their kin." He continues, "all such theories are to be rejected unless they can prove to have historical bases," until further light is had upon the subject we must consider the Negro too, or Sudanese, the proto-Hamite and the fair skinned Hamite are a typical genuine African Race."

All Africans belong to one race and the ties of African brotherhood is more closely united together as one people than any portion of the globe.

They are not Negroes, they are Ethiopians and so is their descendants in America, Asia, Australia, and the East Indies and the Pacific Islands.

Some Anthropologists say that the African Negroes are derived from the face of the chain of Mt. Atlas; they are however, named simply, the Ethiopian Race, from the Ethiopian who were the only black people known to the ancestor in very remote times?

"The word alone had done the race more harm in forty-six years, than two hundred and fifty years of bondage, because it has nothing in its background but slavery and the wilds of the African jungles."

The term Negro has enabled the author of books on Negro life who belong to other races to misclassify the race and to make then separate groups from the great nations of Africa who were the founders of civilization, government, law, and religion; because the word Negro has no historical background to the primitive tribes in Africa, it has completely destroyed the race pride and African culture in the American Negro, the Ethiopian-Italian War did more to revive race pride and race consciousness in America than anything within the past five hundred years.

I noticed and became very interested in reading a book written by Professor Mellville J. Herskovits, professor of anthropology at Northwestern University the title of the book, *The Myth of the Negro Past.*

I felt very fortunate in finding such a book because it verified the contention of my argument on the word Negro. Prof. Harkovits follows the same school of thought and makes the same blunder that is made by most American and European writers.

The word within itself conceals the background of the black man's history. While the book as a whole is very interesting, especially the first chapter titled. "The Significance of Africanism," in this chapter, he gives food for thought and he reaches the highest point toward a solution of the so-called race problem which I consider has yet been written since the days of *Uncle Tom's Cabin.*

But the thing that destroys his high tone of thought is the caption, page 2. "The Negro is thus a man without a past" and in the chapter of his conclusion he repeats the same headline. "The Negro is thus a man without a past."

I must say candidly that professor Herkovit's book has some real merit there are some vital facts in his volume which will be worthy for Negroes to know. But otherwise the term "The Myth of the Negro Past" and the caption, "The Negro is thus a man without a past." I shall now make a direct reply.

The word, "Negro" within itself has no past but slavery the very period that gave it birth.

The term "Negro" as I said before, meant Black Moor; but the term has been converted to mean a separate group of Africans—the most inferior to all races of mankind and who from time immemorial have been slaves and have never been able to rise above the environments of servitude.

The Spanish term was Negro Moor, but the term Moor was eliminated for in short Negro just as Spain or Portugal was formerly known as Iberian Ethiopia.

Modern geography eliminated the word Ethiopia and called it the Iberian Peninsula. So there is no such Race as Negro upon the face of the earth. The word within itself has caused the other races to disrespect the black race and has even caused the black man to lose pride within himself.

The term Negro or Black Moor has been converted to another meaning with the brand of inferiority and underscored by evolution in order to destroy the race heritage in history.

Rev. F. Freeman in his book: "Plea for Africa," says: "In defiance of all records of antiquity whether sacred or profane and equally regardless of evidence which our own times may furnish the Africans are often mentioned as a distinct order of beings, a grade between man and brute."

Dr. Freeman was a great friend to the Negro race and rendered much service to the American colonization society. His volume, "Plea for Africa," is one of the greatest, I have read in Negro history written in 1826 and yet our modern writers do not know or are too timid to state true facts about the black man.

As long as the term Negro is used by anthropologist, historians and these books find their way into libraries, schools, colleges, and universities. The world, especially America, will be misinformed about the history of one of the noblest races that ever lived, that is the true history of the black race.

Volume upon volume have been written by authors giving a false conception of the black man's history and no colored author has yet met the challenge.

I claim that I have met it: There is no such race as Negro and the word Negro has no place in the science of ethnology. Prichard says in his *Natural History of Man,* Vol. 1, page 319: "Nothing has tended more to spread vague and false notions in subjects connected with ethnology than the improper use of general names."

It has often been a question what races among the inhabitants of Africa are Negroes, the meaning of the term not being defined. It ought to be remembered that the word Negro is not a national appellation, but denotes the ideal type constituted by the assemblance of certain physical characteristics which are exemplified in the native in Guinea, in western Africa and their descendants in America and the West Indies.

Notice Prichard's conclusion: "When the characters are not all found, it has often been said African nations though black and nearly black and wooly hair are not Negroes."

One can readily judge what the term Negro applies to—it is slavery. The word Negro is not a racial name, it is an ideal which means that one imagines or wants a thing to be. The term only means African cheap labor as the word "coolie" is applied to Chinese and Malayan workers in South East Asia.

I hope that you have noticed particularly Prichard's definition of Negro—that the word Negro denotes the ideal type constituted by the assemblage of certain characters, which is exemplified in the natives of Guinea in Western Africa and their descendants in America and West Indies.

One can readily see that Prichard's definition of Negro only means those who were captured and sold into slavery, and the section of West Africa from whence they come they are still classified by modern writers as Negroes, the writer continues in the same paragraph with a more explicit definition when he says: "When these characters are not all found it has often been said African nations thought black and nearly black, with wooly hair, are no Negroes."

The above statement shows how abusive the Negro term is.

The question now under consideration is: What is a Negro? They describe the Negro as being black, having wooly hair and thick lips—yet they say the Ethiopians who have black skin and wooly hair are not Negroes. The word Negro has been converted to mean an inferior class or race of people. It does not mean today what the Spanish meant it to be.

I have often heard some would-be race leaders say the word Negro is a healthy name and all that is needed is to spell with a capital letter, but I do not care how you spell it, it means nothing and less than nothing.

The words, Negro and Nigger are twins, born out of race prejudice. There is no such race. The term Negro had no place in Ethnology.

R. C. Lathan in his book, "Man and his Migration," says on page 158-9: "The word Negro means the combination of wooly hair, with a jetty skin, thick lips, narrow forehead, acute facial angle and prominent jaw. It applies to Africans as widely different from each other as the Laplander is from the Eskimo or the Englishman from the Finlander."

If this be the case, the term has no place in Ethnology except so far as its extensive use makes it hard to abandon.

Its real application is to anthropology wherein it

[136]

means the effects of certain influence upon certain inter-tropical Africans irrespective of descent but not irrespective of physical condition, as truly as a short and light skin coincide with the occupancy of mountain ranges, the Negro physiogonomy coincide with that of the Alluvia of River.

Few writers are less desposed to account for ethnological differences by reference to a change of physical location rather than original distinction.

Dr. Daniel, nevertheless expressly states that "when you have the low swamps of the Delta for the Negro, in the sandstone country of the interior, the skin becomes fairer and black becomes brown and brown becomes yellow."

I mention the above quotation to show the cause of the different shades of color found among the races of Africa, which is due solely to climatic influence of low lands and mountain ranges and not to a different species of the race.

Prichard says: "That one may travel from Egypt to Cape Town and see different shades of complexions without observing the break in complexion which change gradually from light yellow, brown to black but they are Ethiopian brothers from a common ancestors. So the Negro only means slavery and not race.

Slavery in Latin America was a matter of cheap labor but in Anglo-Saxon North America was made a matter of Race and today the ghost still haunts us.

Oscar Perchel in his *Races of Men,* page 463. "It is to be regretted that in the opinion certain mistaken Ethnologists, the Negro was the ideal barbarous and beastlike creature. The Negro was said to have a flat forehead, smart like jaws, swollen lips, broad flat nose, short crisp hair falsely called wool, long arms and flat feet.

No single tribe, however, possesses all these deficiencies. The colors of the skins progress through every graduation from ebony black to the light tint of Mulattoes, copper colored, on some tribes; the nose is pointed straight or hooked even Grecian profile.

Traveler says with surprise that they can not find anything of the so-called Negro type among Negroes.

12

The United States of Africa

"Princes shall come out of Egypt; Ethiopia shall soon stretch out her hands unto God" Psalms 68:31.

The only hope of solution for the Negro Problems of America and Africa, is for the United Nations with America and England playing the leading role, to divide the African Continents into separate sections, so that the blacks and whites may live there within their own zones of influence and that each may live his own life and worship God beneath their own vine and fig tree.

Much has been done for the oppressed Nations of Europe for France, Belgium, Poland, Greece, China, the Philippines and India, our men are dying upon a hundred battle fields on the farflung Fronts of the world for "a DEMOCRACY" which is denied the Black Race in America and his Blood Brothers in their Father land Africa.

The recent Race Riots in Detroit and New York, lynchings in the South and current race friction through the Nation in the midst of the greatest and gravest war in human history, are evidence of one fact: that if the Colored race is to be protected from mob violence, economic handicaps, race riots and all social injustices, they must create their own social order and build their own National Life.

The same conditions of segregation and explorations that confronts the race in America, exist among the Colonial Powers in Africa on a much larger scale, and, I am only asking the Great Powers of the World for a Place where Black Men may live in their own Homeland FREE AND UN-MOLESTED by racial prejudices and economic handicaps.

The Race Problem in America has become a political and social racket and I say in all frankness of soul, mind and heart the many books on this subject do not even touch the surface of the problem.

The only Solution is Self Determination upon the part of the Negro to build for himself and posterity, a New World, if the Black race of America and Africa is to survive after this great Catastrophe. It must rise to take its place as a Nation among the other Nations of the earth and their rights respected by all Men.

You hear that some of the so called friends of the Black Race and also some of its own racial leaders remark that "The Negro race in America has made the greatest Progress of any race in the world, since its Emancipation."

But this is not true in any sense of constructive reasoning, such a statement has not one leg to stand on, it's an air castle expression, or like a house built upon the sand, only waiting for the floods to descend and it will be washed away.

[140]

Racial Progress is rated by its industrial and economic assets, such as trade, commerce, political influence and power; the Negro possessed none of these essentials, but none of these are beyond his attainments, the race is handicapped by the American dual system of society which forces each race to make its progress in separate units, this is utterly impossible to do while living in the same community and country without a conflict of interest, the competition is too great.

The only solution to these conditions is Land Grant Territory. The race was emancipated after having toiled and worked as slaves for nearly two hundred and fifty years and turned loose without a dime or a foot of land.

The Race has never been given Territory but instead they were Emancipated and left on their master's plantations, a man is never free on another man's ground.

The Establishment of a Negro Nation on the African Continent would not mean that all Negroes would be compelled to go there, but it would be open for those who desire to go and build a Nation for themselves just as the Pilgrim fathers came to America with the Blue Print of an empire and began this Nation.

Such a Movement would serve as an outlet for the ambitious of the youth of the Race who are now being educated here without a future.

Such Industrial Colleges as Tuskegee in Alabama, Hampton, Virginia, Tennessee State, Mississippi Industrial and a hundred other schools and colleges throughout America could train the Colored Youth to do pioneer work in the Building of this New Nation.

Such Program, to begin with would revise the System of Negro Education with a Racial Back Ground of its own history.

Today the Colored youth is educated to know more about the history and achievements of all races but their own.

The Colored youth need a different slant on the History of his own race in Africa. Today they are being educated as Negroes yet there is no such race found on the Pages of ancient History, the word was formerly used by the Spanish slave trader meaning Black Moor and later became the "Trade Mark" of the slave traffic but it has no anthropological setting in history. The Black race of America are decendants of the Ethiopians and absolutely they are not Negroes.

This African Nation would be a balance of Power for World Peace and would serve as a great factor to hold in check the rising tides in Asia.

There are over Sixteen hundred million of non-whites in the world today, but the Negro is the only group of darker race that has taken on Western Culture.

The Chinese as a Nation still follow the teachings of Confusius; The Hindoos still bow at the Shrine of Budha, the Japanese believe in Shinto, the Arabs, Turks and Indians still look to Mecca; but the Negroes have mastered, in fifty years, a civilization that took the white man a thousand years to build and they have taken the white man's Religion more seriously than he did. Planting a Negro Nation on the West Coast of Africa, with the Ethiopian Christian Nation on the East Coast would readily bring Africa into the fold of Western Culture and Religion which would eventually overthrow Mohammedan activities on that Continent.

This New African Nation would be a great asset to the markets of America, an educated and cultural Africa would have a far greater purchasing power than the few whites who now live there. The time was never riper than now to launch this Program, the race problem has reached its acute stage both in America and in Africa. The frictions and clashes between whites and blacks have become almost a daily occurence in one section or another throughout the Nation. The Negroes only Solution is Self Determination, that is to build a Nation for themselves.

While I have often heard the remarks that the Negro cannot govern themselves, I have found this to be nothing but Colonial Propaganda, an excuse for exploitation.

Negroes have been governors, Kings, Queens, Princes in Africa for many thousand years. The late Negro Governor General in French Equatorial Africa: Felix Sylvestre Eboue, a full blooded Black Man born in Cayenne, French Guinea, he was Governor of a Province, five times larger than France, that contained an area over one million square miles, one third as large as continental United States.

This Black Governor defied the Axis after Paris and the French Empire in Northern Africa and the East Collapsed, but Eboue stood as a Stonewall Jackson in defiance of the Axis Powers. He swung his strategetical strength to DeGaule and by so doing he saved the British Colonies from Axis penetration.

The great service which Governor Eboue rendered France, the Allies and his black countrymen of Africa, only serves to show the wisdom of what Black Leaders could and would do for the race when given an opportunity.

The following tribute was paid this Noble Governor by Jean De LaRoche of the French Liberation Committee of New York in reviewing his life: "France has lost its greatest colonial adminstrator. He was a great Frenchman, one of the greatest. He could discourse on theology with Catholic or Protestant. His knowledge of philosophy was phenomenal. He knew the best literature of the world, carried the poetry of his country in his colossal memory, spoke English, Spanish, French and was fluent in the language of the three African tribes.

He knew every village in the 1,125,754 square miles under his administration, each chief, and many of their subjects as well, also thousands of white settlers among the six million of inhabitants.

In the midst of prosecuting the war, Eboue maintained light motorized troops financed by his people, both the rich and poor, and he conducted one of the most enlightened colonial programs of modern times.

He began a frontal attack on tropical diseases—increasing the number of physicians from 200 to 3,600 and sent teams of native and French Doctors and corps of Native nurses to clean up infested areas.

He opened schools for the instruction of the Natives as Medical Aides and Midwives, and inaugurated a system of public work and sanitation, including control of purification of water supplies."

Sir Harry Johnston, in his book *British Central Africa* page 182 says: "It only remains to say a few words about the relations between the Europeans and the Natives, I am convinced that this Eastern portion of Central Africa will never be a white man's country. Between the Zambezi and the Blue Nile. Africa in the first instance must be governed in the interest of the black man and the blacks will be the race predominant in numbers, if not influence."

The future of Tropical Africa is to be another India, not another Australia—yet Central Africa possesses boundless resources, in the way of commerce, extremely rich in natural products, animals, vegetables and minerals which will pay the Europeans to develop, and equally profit the black man to produce."

A letter from H. M. Stanley, African Explorer in W. Laird Clowes book *Black America,* page 211 says: "There is space enough in one section of the upper Congo Basin to locate doubly the numbers of Negroes in the United States without disturbing a single tribe now inhabiting the country."

"I refer to the immense upper Congo Forest country three hundred and fifty thousand square miles in extent which is three times larger than the Argentine Republic."

Jan Christian Smuts in his book *Toward a Better World,* page 41, says: "If Africa has to be redeemed, if Africa is to make her own contribution to the world, if Africa is to take her place among the continents, we shall have to proceed on different lines and evolve a policy which will not pour her institutions into a European mold. If they live mixed up together it is not practical to sort them out under separate institutions of their own. Institutional segregation carries with it territorial segregation."

Dr. W. B. Dubois in his book *Dark Waters* quotes: "Colored America demands that the return of the conquered German colonies should not be returned to Germany neither held by the Allies. Thousands of colored men sick of White arrogancy and hypocrisy, see in this their race's only salvation."

Bishop H. M. Turner of the A. M. E. Church wrote W. P. Pickett, a letter endorsing Pickett's book, *Abraham Lincoln's Solution of the Race Problem,* says: "I pray God that you may continue the great work you are now engaged in and move this country to help immigrate the Negro to the land of his ancestors. I have visited the country as many times as I have fingers on my hand and it is one of the richest countries under the whole heaven in natural resources. Millions of colored people in this country want to go."

Bishop Wm. D. Chapelle of the African M. E. Church, in his biography says: "I have believed, and now believe, that Ethiopia shall stretch forth her hands to God: that the American Negro, through the Religious Zeal which the African Methodist Church is fostering, and racial pride which education and proper understanding ought to prepare him mentally, morally and financially to go to his kinsman on African soil and intermingling business and marriage, develop the Negro to degrees of attainment undreamed by us."

History of Mankind, volume 2, page 257—Ratzell: "It is assumed of a number of African races that they are hybrids hardly one has been designated by all observers as wholly pure and even when we consider those which have sprung up in historical times from the combination of known elements no other portion of the earth offers so many, so large, and so influential hybrids races; the Moors to the North, the Sudanese to the South of the Desert, the Swajelis in the East, and the Bastaards in the South, and in this it is not merely a case of little drop of African blood but it takes the first place; we must not call it Europeanization or Arabinazation, but Negronization. On the East coast this process can be observed in the descendants of Arabs, on the West in those of Portugese and Negro women. Similarly the population of the Libyan, Desert of Fezzan, even of Morocco itself, is in a fair way to become Negro. It is their numbers that the historical force of the African has hitherto lain. Masses of them have been thrown on the coast of Asia, America and even Europe. In America the whole Island as San Domingo and Jamaica, have fallen to the Negro; several States of the union, as well as Nicaragua, show Negro majorities, and in Brazil all classes are permeated by the Negro elements, as a rule, indeed, they have remained patiently in lower walks of life, thereby not belying the basis of their historical character. Their capacity for education,

[147]

however, is in results that may, at perhaps no very remote epoch, materially alter our judgment as to the capacity and historical destiny of the stock. In our day Africa has become the scene of a great movement, which must fix its destiny in history for thousands of years, while a century ago the great political and trading powers were still merely hanging on like leeches to its outskirts, today the "spheres of interest", domains of power of which the extent is not yet known even to their own, are meeting in the far interior of the continent. Herewith for the first time Europeans are coming in close connection with the most vigorous shoot of the dark branch of Nations, on the soil most appropriate to it, but to them in the first place by no means favorable. Now it will be decided whether much or little of these, the oldest of all now living stocks, will press into the mankind of the remotest of future. And that is one of the greatest problems of the history of the world, which must be the history of mankind."

The United States of Africa, a Prophecy

In the Volume called THE PROGRESS OF RACE (31), edited by Professor J. H. Crogman, Booker T. Washington and J. W. Gibson says: "unless the Negro out of Africa, goes to Africa seeking a Home because he has none, goes on his volition with a correct knowledge of Africa, if my opinion of the future were asked, says Heli Chatalain, I should not hesitate to declare my conviction that within a hundred years all the Bantu-Land will contain more than Five hundred million inhabitants, will equal Europe in civilization, will be united in a great UNITED STATES OF CENTRAL AFRICA, under a new and improved condition of our American Constitution, will both speak and write a common language, the Mother tongue of the Bantu dialects as revised by scholars and enriched by the best development of its daughters, will produce masterpieces of literature, science and art, vying with all the best that Europe and America will then be able to bring forth."

Therefore I am asking in the Name of the Almighty God for the united Nations to include within their Peace covenant a Territorial Grant of Four Million Square Miles of Territory to be set apart on the West Coast of Africa with a full outlet to the sea, including the former German Colonies in East and West Africa, be set apart as an exclusive domain for the Ethiopian Race and to be known as the United States of Africa.

This International State would solve the Race problem in America and would in the meantime emancipate the Natives from four hundred years of slavery, serfdom and exploitation by Colonial Powers which has been a curse to the Continent.

It would be the fulfillment of the Prophecy: that "Ethiopia would stretch out her hands unto God and then Liberia would become another Plymouth Rock where Pilgrims yet may land where the Color of man's skin will not be a bar to his ambition."

13

Summary of the Ethiopian Emperors Address

The Courtesy of Pennsylvania State Library
GENEVA, June 30.—Following is a summary of
the address before the League of Nations Assembly
today by Emperor Haile Selassie of Ethiopia, with
the principal parts given textually:

"I, Haile Selassie I, Emperor of Ethiopia, am here
today to claim that justice which is due to my people
and the assistance promised it eight months ago,
when fifty nations asserted that aggression had been
committed in violation of international treaties.
None other than the Emperor can address the appeal
of the Ethiopian people to those fifty nations.

"There is no precedent for the head of a State
himself speaking in this assembly, but there is also
no precedent for a people being the victim of such
injustice and of being at present threatened by
abandonment to an aggressor.

"Also there has never before been an example
of any government proceeding with the systematic
extermination of a nation by barbarous means in
violation of the most solemn promises, made to all
the nations of the earth, that there should be no re-

sort to a war of conquest and that there should not be used against innocent human beings terrible poison and harmful gases.

"It is to defend a people struggling for its age-old independence that the head of the Ethiopian empire has come to Geneva to fulfill this supreme duty, after having himself fought at the head of his armies.

"Deadly Peril" Is Pictured

"I pray to Almighty God that He shall spare the nations the terrible sufferings that have just been inflicted on my people and of which the chiefs who accompany me here have been the horrified witnesses.

"It is my duty here to inform the governments assembled at Geneva—responsible as they are for the lives of men, women and children—of the deadly peril which threatens them by describing to them the fate which has been suffered by Ethiopia. It is not only upon the warriors that the Italian Government has made war. It has above all attacked populations far removed from hostilities in order to terrorize and exterminate them.

"At the beginning, toward the end of 1935, Italian aircraft hurled upon my armies bombs and tear gas. Their effects were slight. The soldiers learned to scatter, waiting until the wind had slowly dispersed the poisonous gases. Italian aircraft then resorted to mustard gas. Barrels of the liquid were hurled upon armed groups. But this means also was not effective. The liquid affected only a few soldiers and the barrels upon the ground were themselves a warning to the troops and the population of danger.

[151]

"It was when the operations for the encirclement of Makale were taking place that the Italian command, fearing a rout, followed the procedure which it is now my duty to denounce to the world. Special sprayers were installed on board aircraft so they could vaporize over vast areas of territory a fine, death-dealing rain.

Planes Rained Destruction

"Groups of nine, fifteen or eighteen aircraft followed one another so that the fog issuing from them formed a continuous sheet. It was thus that, as from the end of January, 1936, soldiers, women, children, cattle, rivers, lakes and pastures were drenched continually with this deadly rain.

"In order to kill off systematically all living creatures and in order more surely to poison the waters and pastures, the Italian command made its aircraft pass over and over again.

"That was the chief method of warfare. The very refinement of the barbarism consisted in carrying ravage and terror into the most densely populated points in the territory—points the furthest removed from the scene of hostilities. The object was to scatter fear and death over a great part of the Ethiopian territory.

"These fearful tactics succeeded. Men and animals succumbed. The deadly rain that fell from the aircraft made all those whom it touched fly shrieking with pain. All those who drank poisoned water or ate infected food also succumbed in dreadful suffering. In tens of thousands the victims of Italian mustard gas fell.

[152]

"It was in order to denounce to the civilized world the tortures inflicted on the Ethiopian people that I resolved to come to Geneva. None other than myself and my brave companions in arms could bring to the League of Nations the undeniable proofs.

"The appeals of my delegates, addressed to the League of Nations, had remained without answer. My delegates had not been witnesses. That is why I decided myself to come and bear witness against the crime perpetrated against my people and to give Europe warning of the doom that awaits it if it should bow before the accomplished fact."

The Emperor went on to detail what he called the various stages of the Ethiopian drama, ending in his appeal to the League.

"Unhappily for Ethiopia," he continued, "this was at a time when a certain government considered that the European situation made it imperative at all costs to obtain the friendship of Italy. The price paid would be abandonment of Ethiopian independence to the greed of the Italian Government.

"This feature of the agreement, contrary to the obligations of the covenant, has exerted a great influence over the course of events. Ethiopia, and the whole world, have suffered and are still suffering today from its disastrous consequences."

Fulfillment Questioned

"Has each of the State members, as it was its duty to do in virtue of its signature appended to Article XVI of the covenant, considered the aggressor as having committed an act of war personally directed

[153]

against itself? I had placed all my hopes in the execution of these undertakings. My confidence had been confirmed by repeated declarations made in the Council to the effect that aggression must not be rewarded and that force would end by being compelled to bow before right.

"In December, 1935, the Council made it clear that its feelings were in harmony with those of the hundreds of millions of people who, in all parts of the world, had protested against the proposal to dismember Ethiopia. It was constantly repeated that there was not merely a conflict between the Italian Government and Ethiopia, but also a conflict between the Italian Government and the League of Nations, and that is why I personally refused all proposals to my personal advantage made to me by the Italian Government, if only I would betray my people and the covenant of the League.

"I was defending the cause of all small people who are threatened with aggression.

"What is to become of the promises made to me? As long ago as October, 1935, I noted with grief, but without surprise, that three powers considered their undertakings under the covenant as absolutely of no value. Connections with Italy impelled them to refuse to take any measures whatsoever to halt the Italian aggression. On the other hand, it was a profound disappointment to me to learn the attitude of a certain government which, while ever protesting its scrupulous attachment to the covenant, has tirelessly used all its effort to prevent its observance.

"As soon as any measure which was likely to be

rapidly effective was proposed various pretexts were
devised in order to postpone even consideration of
that measure. Did the secret agreements of January, 1935, provide for this obstruction?

"The Ethiopian Government never expected any
other government to shed its soldiers' blood to defend the covenant when their own immediate personal interests were not at stake. The Ethiopian
warriors asked only means to defend themselves.
On many occasions, I have asked for financial assistance for purchase of arms. That assistance has
been constantly refused to me. What then, in prac-
tice, is the meaning of Article XVI of the covenant
and of collective security?

"Finally, statements have just been made in Parliament by the governments of certain powers,
among whom are the most influential members of
the League, that since the aggressors have succeeded
in occupying a large part of the Ethiopian territory,
they propose not to continue application of any of
the economic and financial measures that may have
been decided upon against the Italian Government.

"I assert that the problem submitted to the Assembly today is much wider than merely a question
of settlement of Italian aggression; it is collective
security, it is the very existence of the League. It is
the confidence that each State is to place in international treaties. It is the value of promises to small
States that their integrity and independence shall be
respected and insured. It is the principle of equality of States on the one hand, or otherwise the ob-
ligation made upon small powers to accept the bonds

[155]

of vassalship. In a word, it is international morality that is at stake.

"Apart from the Kingdom of the Lord, there is not on this earth any nation that is superior to any other. Should it happen that a strong government finds that it may, with impunity, destroy a small people, then the hour strikes for that weak people to appeal to the League to give its judgment in all freedom. God and history will remember your judgment.

"Placed by the aggressor face to face with an accomplished fact, are the States going to set up the terrible precedent of bowing before force? Your Assembly doubtless has before it proposals for reform of the covenant and rendering more effective the guarantee of collective security. Is it the covenant that needs reform?

"What undertakings can be of any value if the will to keep them is lacking? It is international morality which is at stake, and not the articles of the covenant.

"Of the powers who have promised to guarantee the collective security of small States and who raise the threat that they may one day suffer the fate of Ethiopia, I ask: What measures do you intend to take? Representatives of the world, I have come to Geneva to discharge in your midst the most painful of duties for the head of a State. What reply have I to take back to my people?"

14

The Negro in Contemporary History

It has often been said that the Negro is an inferior race, and that in many respects, so far as racial solidarity is concerned, he is at the lowest level. On the other hand you will frequently hear that the Negro has made the greatest progress within the first fifty years of his emancipation than has any other race in that short space of time. Both of these above statements have no basic facts. The Negro is far being an inferior people, but if there were such a thing as a superior race, the Negro woul head the list. He is the oldest survival of the human race and the parent stock of all nations. The Negro gave to the world its science, art, religion, and Culture. The modern world to-day is but a reproduction of what has been. "There is nothing new under the sun" what we see, and hear to-day is only an improvement or an evolution from the things of the past.

As to his progress since Freedom, it has been exaggerated. The first Negroes did not come to America as savages, as histories have described them; while it was never the less true, that there were some from among the primitive tribes that were brought with the more civilized ones. But the rank and file of the Africans were as much civilized when they first came to America as the men that bought them.

During the slave period there were more outstanding leaders, more authors and poets in proportion to the population at that time, than there have been found among the race since its Emancipation. In fact the greatest men the race has produced came out of the Slave Period; but here I would like to be distinctively understood, that being a slave was not the cause of their development—Slavery is a curse to any people; but it was their African Culture and tradition that was handed down from one generation to the other, which gave inspirations to the greatest Leaders that the Race has produced during its Sojourn in America.

The Negro came here with a culture of many thousand years. He is the only race that has been Contemporary to all history.

Albert Hooten Professor of Anthropology at Harvard University in his Book "Up from the Ape" Page 592, says: "Archaeology has brought to light on the banks of the Niger in West Africa, in the upper part of the Nile Valley and in Rhodesia (South Africa) extensive monumental remains of great and extinct civilizations which seem to have been Negroid.

"In historical times Negroes have built up both in East and West Africa, powerful and well organized kingdoms which merit the name of civilization."

[158]

He further says: "If one is to credit the white with every cultural achievement made by the white or any race of mixed origin styled white, the same latitude must be extended to the Negro, under such interpretation a large share of the great civilization of India must be assigned to the Negro for a very strong strain of Negro blood is found in India's Population."

Every time that God has made a great man of any race, he has also made a Great Black Man to keep him company.

King Nimrod the Builder of the great City of Babylon and founder of the Babylonian Empire, was a Black Man.

Josiah Priest in his Book American Antiquities (Page 56), says: "The Septuagint version of the Scriptures speaks of Nimrod as being a surly Giant; this was a Colored Man and the first Monarch of the human race after the Flood."

When Abraham pitched his tent on the plains of Sodom, Melchesdek, the Black Priest Ordained him.

When Moses led the Children of Israel out of Egypt, Jethro his Ethiopian Father-in-Law, aided him in the Exodus.

When Solomon built the Temple at Jerusalem, Her Majesty the Queen of Sheba, was his Royal Guest. Josiah Priest's American Antiquities (page 36), says: "The Queen of Sheba was of this race, who came as it is said from the uttermost parts of the earth to Jerusalem to know the Wisdom of Solomon, (She) being a decendant of Ham's Posterity, was a Black Woman."

When the Infant Christ was born in Bethlehem

of Judea, one of the Wise men of the East who visited the Manger, was the Black King Kasper of Tyre.

The Black Simeon of Cyrene, lifted the Cross from burdened shoulders of the Son of God and bore it to the summits of Calvary.

Among the early Converts to the New Testament Church, was an Ethiopian Eunuch, the Treasurer of Queen Candance of Ethiopia.

When Rome produced her Scipio Africanus, Carthage, an African Nation, produced her Hannibal who has been rated as one of the greatest generals of all time.

One of the great Caesars of Rome was an African Ruler, whose name was Septemius Severius who was a Carthagian by birth and Nationality, in honor of his Fatherland, he ordered the Statue of Hannibal to be erected in the Square at Rome. Severius led army of invasion in England to subdue uprising Britons, he died of pneumonia at York, England 210 A. D.

When France produced her Napoleon, Black Haiti, produced Tousaint L'Overture who defeated Napoleon's Army before Wellington fought the Battle of Waterloo. America has her George Washington, the Father of his Country; Black America has its Booker T. Washington, the Father of Industrial Education.

When America produced Stephen A. Douglas with his Doctrine of Squatter Sovereignty, the Black Race produced Frederick Douglas, the Statesman and the Morning Star of their Emancipation.

It was Scotland's Robert Burns who wrote of

his "Highland Mary". But it was the Black Poet Dunbar who wrote "When Malindy Sings".

It was Stephen Foster who wrote: "My Old Kentucky Home," but it was James Bland, the Colored Singer who gave us: "Carry Me Back to Old Virginia".

In the Sports world there is Jack Johnson the Pugilist, who defeated Jim Jefferies. When Germany produced her Schmelling, the Black race produced Joe Louis. The late George Washington Carver, as a Scientist, Marion Anderson as a Singer, Roland Hays, another Master of Song. Paul Robeson in Dramatic Art. have reached the ceiling of their professions.

When Europe produced her saber rattling Mussolini and Hitler, Ethiopia produced His Majesty King Haile Selassie who was the first to draw his Sword in the defense of World Democracy and the first of the exiled Kings to return to his Throne. Sir Harry Johnston in his Volume of Interracial Problems (Page 335-36) says: "The Negro is the only Non-Caucasian Race which has so far furnished rivals to the white man in science, arts, literature, and mathematics; but such races as the Japanese, American Indians and other people of Asia, Africa, Oceania have kept to themselves and have never ventured to compete with the white man in his sphere.

There are famous Negroid poets, musicians, novelists, botanists, philosophers, mathematicians, engineers and general officers whose work is done in the white world and in competition with first talent of Europe and America."